On Durkheim's Rules of Sociological Method

On Durkheim's Rules of Sociological Method

Mike Gane

ROUTLEDGE
London and New York

First published in 1988
by Routledge

First published in paperback in 1989
by Routledge
11 New Fetter Lane, London EC4P 4EE
29 West 35th Street, New York, NY 10001

Set in 10/12pt Sabon,
and printed in Great Britain
by Butler and Tanner Ltd,
Frome & London

Library of Congress Cataloging in Publication Data
Gane, Mike.
    On Durkheim's rules of sociological method.

    Bibliography: p.
    Includes index.
    I. Sociology—Methodology.   2. Durkheim, Emile,
1858–1917.   I. Title.
HM24.G287   1988   301'.01'8   87–23556

British Library CIP Data also available
ISBN 0-415-04252-6

Contents

Preface vii
Acknowledgments ix
Abbreviations of Titles xi

PART ONE

1 Durkheim, the *Rules* and the Problem 1
2 The Remarkable Argument of the *Rules* 12
3 The Problematic Consistency of Durkheim's 'Official' Method 21
4 Variations of Method in Durkheim's Main Sociological Analyses 43
5 Durkheim's Sociology 59

PART TWO

6 Introduction: the *Rules* and the Sociologists 67
7 The Debate Over the *Rules* in Recent British Sociology 69
8 The Storm Over the *Rules* in France During Durkheim's Lifetime 75
9 French Discussions of the *Rules* After 1917 87
10 The Anglo-Saxon Reception of the *Rules* 93
11 Durkheim's Brief Reply to his Critics 103

PART THREE

12 Complex Transitions 107
13 A Closer Look at the Emergence of the *Rules* 126
14 An Examination of the Argument of the *Rules* 137
15 Criticisms of Durkheim Examined 151
16 Conclusions 171

Bibliography 184
Name Index 189
Subject Index 191

We must make therefore a complete solution and separation of nature, not indeed by fire, but by the mind, which is a kind of divine fire.

(Bacon, 1620)

Preface

This book began its life as a critical essay and its aim has remained essentially a modest one. Far from being an attempt to construct a finished methodological treatise or to present a definitive commentary on Durkheim's *Rules*, methods, or – even more ambitious – on the methods of the Durkheimian school, its central objective is to put into question some general and strongly persisting misconceptions of Durkheim's research strategies.

It is certainly something of a paradox that Durkheim's short book, *The Rules of Sociological Method*, acknowledged as a classic and available in two English translations, is both widely read yet seems to remain in some vital respects unknown. Even the most apparently authoritative considerations of its arguments seem to me quite perverse. The reasons for this state of affairs interest me in their own right, and I devote some attention to trying to work out precisely how the text has been read. The generally dire level of the discussion of this text has meant that much of the debate on its arguments has either been polarised in fixed awkward positions, or simply gone round in circles.

In this book I try to begin to argue, by working from some of the often neglected aspects of Durkheim's text, that the work is more complex and challenging than is currently assumed. I must confess to a curious sense of unease when I have felt irritation over naive criticisms of this work since I am not a 'Durkheimian' in the pure sense. There is nothing, however, to be gained by oversimplifying Durkheim's arguments in order to demolish them; yet obviously, there is some insufficiency simply in presenting the 'real' argument, even if it is salutary for sociologists to have to face up to it. I therefore try to open out and discuss the remarkable ingenuity of this short work and to try to discover the way in which it works as a unified and unifying sociological manifesto. Further: analyses of Durkheim's work, I suggest, which fail to take into account the perspectives in which the *Rules* was shaped, seem unable to grasp the key elements of Durkheim's project.

Acknowledgments

I first encountered Durkheim's work as a first year undergraduate in sociology at Leicester University in 1965. In many direct and indirect ways this essay on the *Rules* owes a great deal to the intellectual milieu of the Department of Sociology at Leicester, particularly my immediate teachers and fellow students but also other sociologists who were active there in the mid 1960s, and during the year I taught there (1971–2). I have also continued to discuss Durkheimian themes with sociologists who subsequently joined that department. I would also like to thank all those who have participated in discussions at seminars not only at Leicester but also Birmingham, Essex, Hull, Keele; and the many colleagues and students at Loughborough University with whom I have discussed problems raised in this book. A number of my papers on Durkheim and Mauss have been published in the journal *Economy and Society* and I would like to thank the editors for providing critical and constructive observations. I have also had considerable help from Monique Arnaud, who not only helped with translating some of Durkheim's passages into English, but also provided critical responses to some of my initial ideas.

Abbreviations of Titles

Division published as *De la Division du Travail Social: Étude sur l'Organisation des Sociétés Supérieures*, 1st ed., 1893, 2nd, 1902; Paris, Alcan. English translations, both entitled *The Division of Labour in Society*, by G. Simpson (1964b 1933)), and W. D. Halls (1984).

Rules published as a set of articles, 'Les Règles de la Méthode Sociologique' in *Revue Philosophique de la France et de l'étranger*, 1894, 1st ed., 1895, Alcan, 2nd ed., 1901, etc. English translations, both entitled *The Rules of Sociological Method*, by S. A. Solovay and J. H. Mueller (1964a (1938)), and W. D. Halls (1982).

Educational Thought published posthumously as *L'Évolution Pédagogique en France*, 1938, PUF; given as lectures in Paris in 1904 as *L'Histoire de l'Enseignement en France*. Translation by P. Collins, entitled *The Evolution of Educational Thought in France: Lectures on the Formation and Development of Secondary Education in France* 1977, Routledge & Kegan Paul.

Elementary Forms (or simply *Forms*) published as *Les Formes Élémentaires de la Vie Religieuse: le Système Totémique en Australie*, 1912, Paris, Alcan. Translation by J. Swain, entitled *The Elementary Forms of the Religious Life*, 1961 (1915), Allen & Unwin.

PART ONE

Man is excentric to himself

(Merleau-Ponty)

1

Durkheim, the *Rules* and the Problem

(i)

Emile Durkheim was born into an eminent Jewish family in eastern France in 1858. His adult life spans the period between the Franco-Prussian War and the First World War. He died in November 1917 at the age of 59.

After studying at the Ecole Normale Supérieure (1879–82), Durkheim taught at a number of Lycées between 1882 and 1887, a period broken by a term's study in Germany, Berlin and Leipzig (1886) before taking up his first University position at Bordeaux where he worked from 1887–1902 (holding the 'Chaire de Science Sociale' from 1896). A second period of fifteen years was then spent at the Sorbonne in Paris 1902–17 (holding the 'Chaire de Science de l'Education' from 1902, and the 'Chaire de Science de l'Education et Sociologie' from 1913). Founder of the famous sociological yearbook, the *Année Sociologique*, and the school of sociology known as the *Année* school, or more simply the Durkheimian school, his stature has grown rather than diminished in sociology in the period since his death, at least outside of France. Today the 'founding fathers' of modern sociology are generally regarded as the trinity: Marx, Weber and Durkheim. Although it would be a gross error to think these are the only influences of any significance on modern sociology, or even its direct progenitors, they are without doubt its most brilliant formative influences. Translations and commentaries of Durkheim's writings, at first only a trickle, have become an inundation.

Many more collections are promised: letters, essays and so on; the flood is not likely suddenly to stop. It must be noted that many of the translations are rather poor, even the more recent ones, and although the recent second translations are more readable than the earlier ones, they are by no means free of error.

This judgment also applies to the work under consideration here, *The Rules of Sociological Method* first published in 1894. Close analysis of the text therefore can only adequately be achieved by checking against the French, especially in key passages, since errors such as the substitution of 'normal' for 'abnormal' (Durkheim, 1982: 98, line 14 up), 'induction' for 'deduction' (p. 150, line 20), 'observations' for 'sensations' (p. 81, line 15 up), can clearly sink any unwary reader.

But it may come as a different kind of surprise for some readers to learn that although this work features prominently on sociology courses very few sociologists outside Durkheim's immediate circles have ever explicitly attempted to use them. Perhaps even this formulation involves a misunderstanding. Anthony Giddens (1976: 8), is right to insist that method here should not be confused with techniques of recording and analysing empirical materials, often taught in sociology as sociological 'method'. The book is much broader than any discussion of, say, survey techniques might suggest. It deals with questions concerning the conceptualisation of social structures and relations between them in the context of the classification of societies, as well as how to engage in sociological analysis of a whole range of social phenomena from family structure to religious ritual. In this context it is significant that a work such as Steve Fenton's *Durkheim and Modern Sociology* (1984) contains virtually no discussion of method or the influence of the *Rules*, and W. S. F. Pickering's *Durkheim's Sociology of Religion* does not directly relate the project of the *Rules* to Durkheim's development of the sociology of religion – and is content to assert that the *Rules* is 'full of serious defects in many people's eyes and shows a very limited knowledge of scientific procedure' (Pickering, 1984: 288). R. A. Jones, in his recent *Emile Durkheim*, again reiterates Lukes's criticisms, adding that the *Rules* 'is Durkheim at his worst' (Jones, 1986: 77). If the *Rules* seems to have become an embarrassment one might ask why it still occupies such a privileged place in the sociological pantheon: should not sociologists simply remove this text and forget about it rather than denounce this apparently meretricious work annually in introductory courses?

(ii)
What may be a suitable way of avoiding the obvious pitfalls of such a negative response? I suggest it is possible and productive to maintain that in some cases an author's way of writing may be compared to his or her way of reading. To understand one is often a helpful step in attempting to illuminate and understand the other. And if, as here, we are aiming to understand the project of which the *Rules* is a part, it is logical that we should pose the question of how Durkheim himself expected and insisted his readers read his own works.

Let us for a moment briefly examine speculatively what this method of reading texts would involve. It would certainly be holistic in the sense that it would aim to move from the whole to the part – impossible of course unless the reader install certain suspensions; this would also imply the proper contextualisation of argument on the one hand, but also the recognition of the reality of the part *vis-à-vis* the context on the other. That this is without doubt Durkheim's position can be seen in the following comment which comes from the first page of the *Rules*:

> If the search for paradox is the mark of the sophist, to flee from it when the facts demand it is that of a mind that possesses neither courage nor faith in science.
> Unfortunately it is easier to accept this rule in principle or theory than to apply it consistently. We are still too used to deciding all such questions according to the promptings of common sense to exclude the latter easily from sociological discussion. Whilst we believe ourselves to be emancipated from it, it imposes its judgments upon us unawares. Only a sustained and special practice can prevent such shortcomings. We would ask the reader not to lose sight of this. (trans mod.)

The reader:

> should always be conscious that the modes of thought with which he is most familiar are adverse rather than favourable, to the scientific study of social phenomena, so that he must consequently be on his guard against first impressions. If he yields to these without resistance he may well have judged our work without having understood us. (Durkheim, 1982: 31–2)

But what should happen if the reader encounters apparent contradiction? One writer has expressed it thus: 'Durkheim might have said "I contradict myself? Very well, I contradict myself!" ' (Nisbet, 1965: 28). Another, more recently:

It would not be difficult to quote passages from Durkheim which seem to contradict each other. When one finds such apparent contradictions in a thinker of Durkheim's magnitude, however, more often than not it indicates that one has not understood him. (Schmaus, 1985: 26–7)

This comment brings into the open what might be called a specifically Durkheimian problem: the moral and intellectual status of the author and ritual attitudes which accompany reading (see the discussion in Goffman, 1981: 187). If other writers conclude easily that Durkheim's efforts are to be rejected because of ambiguity, inconsistency and contradiction, this no doubt in part reflects the character of their opinion of him as a thinker. (A similar point is raised in review of the work of Durkheim's nephew, Mauss, where the reviewer is content to identify apparently opposing lines of thought and immediately concludes that Mauss is simply a rather odd writer housing blatantly inconsistent opinions (Wood, 1978). Such a view comes very close to suggesting that the work is less than sane.) Here, I think it necessary to raise the question more directly as to what Durkheim's own view was. There seems to be little doubt that he regarded reality as inherently complex and therefore any adequate thought, especially in the social sciences, had to reflect that complexity. This could give rise to the notion that any adequate reflection is 'eclectic' or a series of 'mutually exclusive' oppositions. This is illusory, he said, because it is purely abstract. If the elements are understood as part of a complex reality, that is 'in their various places' in that reality, such apparent contradiction evaporates (Durkheim, 1953: 62).

It is essential, in order to follow this kind of complex thinking as a reader, to note qualifications and caveats, some of which may be presented in an extremely modest way. For example, in the Preface to the *Rules* Durkheim counters the suggestion that his position is materialist by stressing that: 'Our method is in part only an application of (the spiritualist) principle to social facts' (Durkheim, 1982: 32). Here the important words are 'in part'. One writer, Bouglé, completely overlooked the qualification and hence easily reached the conclusion that Durkheim was a spiritualist: he cited a passage from Durkheim as follows: 'Society is not a system of organs and functions ... it is the centre of a moral life' (Durkheim, 1953: xl). The actual passage is: 'Society was presented as a system of organs and functions ... Society however, is more than this, for it is the centre of a moral life' (1953: 90–1).

So two conjoint rules must be applied: each argument must be located in an adequate contextualisation, and each caveat, however small, must be given its due. No doubt these observations are only a beginning; but they do suggest that Durkheim's work is written in such a way that we may have to alter the way we normally read if we are to succeed in grasping it.

(iii)
Many of the most serious difficulties in understanding Durkheim stem, it seems to me, from a failure to take this requirement seriously, but even those who have noticed this remarkable aspect of his work do not realise its scope or its consequences. For example, Ernest Wallwork, citing the judgment of Henri Peyre, certainly seemed to have seen this element, which he called Durkheim's dialectic and which he thought 'intense and vital, ambiguous and adventurous, characteristics which make his position on any issue difficult to grasp' (Wallwork, 1972: 6). All Wallwork seems to mean by this, however, is that Durkheim was both a conservative ('in the best sense') and a radical at the same time. This assessment, however inadequate as we shall see, is far superior of course to those which have castigated Durkheim as an arch conservative, or as a naive liberal. Even Giddens's comment that 'in political temper and in sociological conviction Durkheim was an opponent of revolutionary thought' (in Durkheim, 1986: 24), fails to grasp the fact that within his work it is possible to find not only justifications for revolutions but a theory which makes vast collective effervescences the decisive formative moments in social development – further, for Durkheim, society did not simply 'evolve' into existence, it was born in such revolutionary effervescences. Many argue that Durkheim was a political moderate whose limited political horizon was the mediocre French Third Republic; but this overlooks the fact that Durkheim called not only for greater equality but argued that 'so long as there are rich and poor from birth, there can exist no just contract, nor any just distribution of social status' (Durkheim, 1984: lv). And at the end of the *Elementary Forms* he reiterated the judgment that European societies were in a critical moral state and that:

> the state of incertitude ... cannot last forever. A day will come when our societies will know again those hours of creative effervescence ... though the work of (the French Revolution) may have miscarried, it enables us to imagine what might have happened in other conditions; and everything leads us to believe that it will be taken up sooner or later (Durkheim, 1961: 475–6).

5

In other words it is possible to identify in Durkheim's work revolutionary egalitarian themes, and it is perhaps surprising that a coherent left-wing Durkheimianism was not developed in France or elsewhere.

The main problem in trying to place Durkheim in any conventional category is that he combined a number of positions in an unusual way: he opposed anarchism and communism while supporting democratic socialism but refused to subordinate the independence of sociology as a science to any political organisation. While arguing that the continuing function of the state was to assist in the development of individual liberties, these liberties were not unconditional, for socialism demanded its own moral discipline. And socialism was for him not something dreamt up as a new utopia, it 'appears part and parcel of the very nature of higher societies' (Durkheim, 1986: 120). Here lies the peculiarity of Durkheim's political thought: his main therapeutic conclusion for modern societies, the restoration of occupational guilds in a new form, suggests in effect that there are in fact only two basic social forms: primal communism and higher socialism, all the other forms are deviations. The structural problems of the advanced societies arise because necessary occupational institutions have been destroyed, so that, from a morphological point of view, these societies are seriously imbalanced – hence they lurch from crisis to crisis, from war to war. Thus his socialism is tinged with the idea of restoration (for guild socialism, significantly described at more than one point as the norm of the bourgeoisie (e.g. Durkheim, 1957: 33–4; 1984: xlviii), had been lost).

The complexity of this kind of theoretical and political social analysis should make us hesitate a little before reaching a judgment, but as Wallwork says, understating the situation, 'caution has not always been exercised' (Wallwork, 1972: 6). Evidently caution alone is not sufficient; what is required is an examination of this type of complex strategic thought and how it is reflected upon by its author. It is not simply Durkheim's 'method' for it is also applied to his method, as we shall see. For the moment it might be conceived as the deeper lying logic of Durkheim's practice, operating behind the formulation of rules of procedure and sociological analysis. But it is not akin to any formal logic. It seems in fact more like a quasi-political element within the processes which orient the sociological enterprise, in the sense that it appears to be the framework which governs the way choices of analytical policies are made and followed through; it appears as dialectic when Durkheim begins a critique of former positions or available definitions; it appears as policy formation when Durkheim describes the reasons for undertaking a series of tasks in a certain order. The two sides of this practice could be called technique and strategy, and as such form the deeper framework for considerations of projects in epistemology and method. My view is that it is essential to grasp the nature of this strategic element in Durkheim's work as it is the key to understanding its dynamic, its apparent inconsistencies, and is the only way in which its truly original elements can be recognised and assessed.

(iv)
Another way, perhaps, of conceiving this 'dynamic' element is to treat it as some kind of devil in the works: it manoeuvres, calculates, but in highly unexpected and seemingly perverse ways. It is not difficult even to imagine it as emanating from a kind of special organ. Certainly one writer saw Durkheim: 'as a sort of automaton of super-human creation, destined endlessly to preach a new Reform, and who concealed within some vital organ, perhaps the brain ... a perpetual system of unanswerable arguments' (Maire, cited by Lukes, 1973: 371).

But if I try to track down the nature of this devil (it is rather more like an imp), it is in order to grasp not a particular 'theory' but the nature of the realignments of a project. It is to place particular analyses in the context of a larger quest and to see them not as summations but as stepping stones of a necessarily sinuous pathway. I do not doubt the validity of sometimes harsh critical assessments of certain analyses as individual finished works, but I suggest that there is another level of criticism which needs to be undertaken, criticism of the larger strategic dimension of programmes of research. And Durkheim's works are eminently suited for a consideration of this problem, indeed as I will attempt to argue, sociologists, by and large, have missed an opportunity to grasp certain of Durkheim's texts, notably the *Rules*, because they have been unable to identify the dynamic unity between its propositions and the growing points of Durkheim's larger project. At best they have seen this text as 'transitional'. But what is not in some sense transitional?

In this perspective I also inquire into the difficult relation between theory, method and programme. My thesis here is that it is in the consideration of 'method' in the widest sense that we encounter elements of the strategic calculations arising from the programme. Sociology comprises theories and methods, but also projects and strategies which motivate them. Durkheim, in the *Rules*, it seems to me, identifies major phases of sociological inquiry to which correspond appropriate techniques of inquiry. Certain rules are defined, but their justification is given not by reference to one single already complete sociological theory, but often to the already given style of work established in the sciences, particularly the biological sciences. There is as a complement a direct, even naive, appeal to maintain faith in the potentialities of scientific as against ideological procedures. Although Durkheim's argument here is of some interest, what is crucial is the rewriting of the rules as research priorities develop. This is clear evidence of the kind of relationship established between the 'devil' and the method invoked to hold it in check, but the remarkable feature of Durkheim's work is that within certain ranges the former completely dominated the latter, overturning expectations with remarkable regularity.

It is certainly not the objective here to attempt to give Durkheim a lesson retrospectively, or to say that his impish imagination should have been disciplined more thoroughly. In my view, without this gremlin Durkheim's works would certainly be less challenging: the creative tensions exist for the same reasons there appear to be inconsistencies. If it is necessary for the purposes of discussion to present a number of résumés of Durkheim's individual works, as is the case in all such investigations, it is not because these works have become generally accepted within the discipline of sociology or because I myself accept them as established verities: these works are now at one stage removed from such commitments. Yet the commitment to the continued significance of their substantive contribution is, as it were, held in suspension while the texts still retain their magical properties.

A NOTE: A MODERN STUDENT'S 'READING' OF THE *RULES*

How do modern British students read the *Rules* today? College and University teachers of sociology, of course, have not only read the work as students themselves but have also been engaged widely in teaching it. Naturally it is rather difficult to eavesdrop on tutorial classes, but we do have the next best thing. In a remarkable piece of fiction, Maurice Roche has written a short but highly amusing and informative dialogue between what appears to be a student and a lecturer (though this is not actually stated) on the *Rules* (1976). The lecturer finds the student a bit of a handful, to put it mildly: the student seems to be able to outwit the lecturer with considerable ease. As the dialogue develops the lecturer seems to be forced to adopt administrative measures to bring the student into line and into silence. But the implications are that there is a certain collusion between Durkheim's text and the lecturer's authoritarianism. There can be little doubt that Maurice Roche has attempted here a critique of Durkheim, and certainly it is clear that the confrontation illustrates many of the current attitudes and indeed even practices developed in relation to reading this text.

Dialogues on the Rules
The lecturer begins, simply, with an attempt to persuade the student to 'begin at the beginning' and to read Durkheim's essay from the beginning. But problems arise immediately when the student says he finds it difficult even to understand the first word in the text: the word 'we' in the phrase 'we are so little accustomed to treat social phenomena scientifically ...' He asks: 'who' precisely 'are we'? And when Durkheim goes on to suggest that certain propositions of the book 'may well surprise the reader' because it uses a scientific method, the student objects strongly that he could not possibly be surprised 'if I discovered that propositions I came across ... did treat such phenomena scientifically', for how could it come as a surprise that phenomena are treated scientifically if this is announced at the beginning of the work in question? The lecturer quickly loses his composure and announces that the session is finished leaving the impression that the student has scored a couple of bull's-eyes.

In the next session the student asks that if Durkheim is proposing a set of rules, are they not to be considered laws to be binding on the community of sociologists? This makes the lecturer distinctly nervous, a response which seems to deepen when the student notes that Durkheim cites language as a key social fact, which 'coercively constrains' the individual who 'uses' it to express thought. 'What's wrong with that?' asks the lecturer apprehensively. First, says the student, is it not a contradiction to propose, as an individual, a set of constraints or rules which includes the idea that constraints come from the group to the individual? Secondly, is not man within language – so that the expression 'use of language' seems to invalidate the notion that language is an externally constraining structure? Hard pressed, the lecturer suggests that Durkheim backtracks and in fact wants coerciveness of social facts to be thought of as something which can be treated as a quality postulated in social relations in order to facilitate social analysis. Sensing the existence of something rather oppressive here, the student comments, wryly, 'the Marquis de Sade rides again!' His persistence again annoys the lecturer. In claiming that Durkheim does seem capable of being able to explain and account for the 'dream' that is his sociological project, he begins to imply this is true also of the lecturer himself. This infuriates the lecturer who imagines, probably correctly, that he is now regarded as a quack.

The sorely-tried lecturer eventually suggests that all the difficulties would probably be resolved if the student would simply read the book. They would then be in a position to reach agreement as to what the book was trying to say. Unfortunately the student is not at all willing to accept such an easy solution. It is, he says, more important 'for us to be able to agree on *how* the book says what it says'. Durkheim himself, he notes, does not seem to be willing or able to reflect on this problem. He seems to take it for granted that as an expert sociologist he can express his thought in one direction – toward the lay reader who is entirely passive – without any difficulty. The lecturer responds with the suggestion that, for the moment, it is sufficient simply to get on to read and know what is in the text. This is what the student now begins to do, reading out the following words: 'so long as sociology remains involved in partisan struggles ... is content to expound common ideas with more logic than the layman, and, consequently presumes no special competence ... it has no right to speak loudly enough to silence passion and prejudice ...' Obviously causing great embarrassment to the lecturer, he is told to 'shut up!!' But the student comes straight to the point: 'what kind of communication situation is it to be offered either monologue or silence?'

Roche's sketch is no doubt meant as a parody. It is nonetheless evocative: a meeting between a bemused, perceptive and insistent student, and a lecturer doing his session on Durkheim for the umpteenth time. To the student, the whole of the Durkheimian project appears horribly self-contradictory: beginning with a series of unreflexive formulations based on thinly-disguised elitist authoritarianism. These elements become an immediate obstacle for the student, who sees in them a threat to the existence of the very education he is seeking. The lecturer, who in the end makes a direct appeal to the student's own common sense, seems in doing so to contradict further Durkheim's ambition to begin a discourse that will transcend common sense through the development of special competence. The authoritarian dimension seems fully exposed. The poor lecturer appears never to have thought about these issues, and seems willing to practise his despotic authority in order to put an end to awkward questions which threaten not only his theoretical understanding but also his educational practice. A link is thus forged between what appears to be the absence of the recognition of the level of the individual experience of persons in Durkheim's theory and a political tendency to authoritarianism.

However much the discussion may appear ludicrous, there are grounds for believing that it does represent not a possible situation but a probable one today.

2

The Remarkable Argument of the *Rules*

The book is a treatise on method as well as an essay in social theory; no profounder one has been written in sociology. (R. A. Nisbet, 1965: 33)

The *Rules* is not a deep work of theory, or meta-theory; nor is it Durkheim's finest work. (S. Lukes, in Durkheim, 1982: 89)

The *Rules*, originally published in 1894, has the distinction of being available in two separate English translations: one, of 1938 (1964a), the other of 1982. Both of these editions have introductions by well-respected social thinkers (George Catlin and Steven Lukes) who suggest that it is valuable to read the *Rules* for purely negative reasons. We can all learn, they suggest, from the mistakes of the essay, for its errors are above all highly instructive. Even so, it is regarded as a classic statement of a distinctive position on method in sociology and has played its part, at a certain stage in the intellectual legitimation of sociology, as an academic discipline by proclaiming the specificity of its project and its right to exist.

The essay is presented by modern commentators, almost unanimously, as a document which points sociology in the wrong direction. The text indeed possesses strange powers, for it seems to call for repeated rounds of denunciation, as if it indicates the wrong direction with admirable conviction, vigour, even plausibility. At one level, perhaps, its arguments meet with support: it is after all a youthful manifesto, it is analytic and comprehensive. It also possesses magisterial ambition, for its project is nothing less than to unify the field of the whole social sciences.

But these qualities themselves ultimately appear to work against the text. For they have been turned around. Then the text now appears as something which can all the more easily become the object of refutations: its errors are valuable because they show the full set of consequences of such a seriously mistaken line of thought. Durkheimian methodology, especially as perceived in our less optimistic, even cynical, modern intellectual climate, becomes something of a 'negative heuristic' for sociology, a route not to take. But, then, curiously, as we shall see, sociologists are not really agreed as to precisely what is wrong with it.

Nevertheless, if I begin with a résumé of the main arguments it is both to introduce them to readers new to them, and to reintroduce them to those who may even be overfamiliar with them. As no résumé is entirely free of in some way introducing an element of selectivity and partiality, I have used the proportions of the detailed contents list which accompanied Durkheim's 1895 edition, sadly omitted from both translations, as a guide. And for the modern sociologist the sections of the arguments are referenced to the two available editions (I: 1964a; II: 1982).

A BRIEF RÉSUMÉ OF THE ARGUMENT OF THE *RULES*

The discussion begins with an attempt to define the domain of sociology and opens with the dramatic question: what are *social* phenomena or facts? These cannot be the phenomena found generally throughout a society since there is no reason in principle to assume they derive from society itself, they may for example be characteristics of individual biology which are found in each individual. These social realities are best thought of as (i) 'exterior' to each individual consciousness considered purely individually and as (ii) capable of exercising a 'coercive' action on individual consciousnesses. These criteria applied to the consideration of constituted social practices and social currents produce, immediately, a field of special study, the facts of which do not fall under the view of any other science. The phenomena thus selected range from familial obligations to systems of language and commerce. They seem to be able to function independently of purely individual action. This conception can be confirmed through an examination of the case of education where the formation of individual character and mentality occurs under the organised pressure of social forces which combine common beliefs, tendencies and practices (I: 1–6; II: 50–4).

An alternative way of characterising a social fact as a specifically social phenomenon is to conceive it as something which can appear as a way of acting or thinking, established in custom or tradition, which constitutes a relatively distinct reality from any of the practices of a single individual; for example, the standard formulas and practices of religion, etc. There are, it is evident, a great many degrees of such disengagement between the crystallised social forms and individual forms of social action. In some cases auxiliary methods (such as statistics) can be used to measure the relatively free currents of social life. But it is still true that these social facts are general because they are social, and, as they are collective forces, 'impose' themselves on individuals who are, as individuals, not in a position to resist them. A social fact may be recognised because it is a socially sanctioned form, or because it offers, in one way or another, a quite determinate resistance to individual wills. Because it is a generality it may also be perceived immediately as a structure which exists with a certain type of independence from any of the 'individual' forms through which it may be realised. The domain of social facts also includes 'ways of being' which impose themselves through morphological structures, for example: population distributions; political divisions; forms of urbanisation. But these are only ways of acting which have become consolidated, and so are not different in principle from ways of thinking, or acting (I: 6–13; II: 54–9).

In attempting to observe social phenomena an essential rule of sociological method is to treat social facts as things. Two comments are essential: (1) all sciences pass through an ideological phase in the process of their formation. While they are in this phase they have not completed the process of disentangling their object of study from popular notions and conceptions, and much of their activity is based on an acceptance of these notions rather than a critique of them. This phase has been excessively prolonged in sociology compared with other sciences and ideological conceptions have retained far greater authority within them as compared with natural sciences. Auguste Comte for example takes as the object of sociology only a very common notion of the continuous, ever growing, perfection of 'humanity'; Herbert Spencer studied 'co-operation' as the essence of social life. But both are, from the start, ideological preconceptions, the ideological bases of which are not examined. The same procedure is found in ethics and political economy. Whether or not, in the final analysis, social life is the development of such notions should not be a prior assumption which in any way influences method. Method should be influenced only by the necessity for science to treat its phenomena as things and to adopt an approach to them which turns them into data for analysis. Even when phenomena appear artificially or conventionally arranged, this appearance should not, in the first instance, be given any privilege: even the most apparently arbitrary and subjective phenomena reveal, on examination, the symptomatic features of objectivity (constancy and regularity). Indeed sociology can well take advantage of this appearance of objectivity in its phenomena which is often denied to psychology (I: 14–31; II: 60–72). (2) There are three direct corollaries of this proposition: (i) systematically discard all 'prenotions' from social science. Only mysticism opposes this rule. (ii) In order to constitute an object of social research it is necessary to group social facts together according to common external characteristics. All definitions should be dominated by the aim of making contact with these selected characteristics and making them independent from already existing common-sense notions. Sometimes this requires the formation of a new terminology, sometimes a redefinition of a common term. (Spencer's conception of the evolution of marriage, for example, comes to erroneous conclusions because it neglects this requirement. Garofalo's idea of crime is also erroneous for the same reason. The very widespread view that primitive societies have no moral system is also based on the same mistake.) It may be objected, however, that to begin with external characteristics is to begin with the purely superficial aspects of reality. This view is mistaken: it is simply not possible to jump over this stage in social investigation. To begin with such external characteristics is to begin to establish a primary contact with the object, and it creates an initial framework (*le premier point d'appui*). This approach in no way constitutes an obstacle to scientific explanation, since the external characteristics of things are indissolubly linked to their inner determinations. (iii) Sociology should strive to base itself on the most objective materials. In order to achieve this the sociologist must study social facts where they present themselves most completely separated from the purely individual forms (I: 21–46; II: 72–83).

The social facts already discussed, however, fall into two separate categories which must be distinguished theoretically: the normal and the pathological. Opposition to the adoption of the scientific method in sociology has, in part, been based on the idea that although science can advise on the means of action it cannot establish ends or goals. In fact, an attempt to classify phenomena analogously to the biological sciences has the enormous advantage of theoretical and practical unification (I: 47–9; II: 85–7). Three points can be made: first, the question of pathology. The criterion commonly used to identify pathological phenomena is whether or not it causes pain. But pain is not the distinctive sign of illness. It can be constituent of the state of normal health. On the other hand the criterion often used which suggests that any state which reduces an individual's chances of survival are pathological overlooks the fact that such chances are indeed reduced during normal childbirth for the mother and during infancy and old age for all individuals, yet these cannot be pathological states. Illness must be distinguished from health as is the normal from the abnormal. Thus in order to apply this consistently it is essential to take age into account when determining whether a fact is normal or not in a given species (I: 50–8; II: 87–93).

Secondly, there is a connection between normality and generality. An explanation of a social fact must account for the way that a phenomenon is bound up with the conditions of existence of the social species under consideration, either as an essential effect of these conditions or as a means by which adaptation can occur. These analyses are necessary when the method of finding the norm through the average condition of the species is impossible; for instance when the species has not completed its full evolutionary development. But this second method cannot be applied at the beginning of a science when knowledge is too limited. Only when the normal condition has been determined can this functional analysis be undertaken (I: 59–64; II: 94–7).

Thirdly, some surprising results appear following the application of these rules. Crime, for example, often appears, in itself, to be a pathological condition. But if the above rules are applied it becomes clear that crime is a normal phenomenon which appears in all healthy societies. If there are indeed normal rates, and abnormal rates of crime this must mean that crime is somehow linked to important constituent features of society itself. Crime is not only a purely contingent or artificial fact, its disappearance may be the sign of social pathology (I: 64–75; II: 97–104).

The distinction, however, between normal and abnormal facts implies a further problem for sociology, the correct classification of distinct species or social types. The old philosophical dilemma of nominalism versus realism can be bypassed by taking the concept of social species as intermediary between the idea of *genus homo* and particular societies (I: 76–8; II: 108–9). First, in order to clarify the nature of the problem it might seem that an exhaustive survey of relevant studies of individual societies should be undertaken. This is not the case. It is crucial that the experimental method be applied in this domain, through the discovery of decisive facts through well constructed theoretical experimentation. Even one such experiment correctly carried out can establish this. In relation to the question of classification, therefore, such experiments must focus on the number, nature and mode of combination of the elements which make up societies (I: 78–81; II: 109–12). Secondly, as Spencer has shown, it is possible to begin a classification from the most basic single segment society, and establish subsequent degrees of complexity, from poly-segmental societies of simple composition to societies of double composition, and so on (I: 81–6; II: 112–15). Thirdly, it must be recognised that this field of social morphology is more complex than the problem of classification in biology, since, in society, the mechanism of heredity does not reside in the organism. Specific types are more difficult to establish (I: 86–8; II: 116–7).

Social morphology is, however, only one element in the process of sociological explanation. A full sociological explanation has to take the following problems into account. Firstly, most forms of explanation in the social sciences follow individual teleology. But this is to overlook the fact that the utility of a phenomenon for individual consciousness does not explain why the social fact exists. The question is complicated by both the fact that social phenomena can persist over a long period of time, and the relative independence over time of the organ and the function it may perform. It is therefore necessary to establish the efficient cause of a social fact, and this is paramount. The function of a social fact may well be easier to determine once its efficient cause is established (I: 89–97; II: 119–25). Secondly, the method of explanation generally adopted is also predominantly psychological, even in Comte and Spencer. Society, however, being a specific level of the organisation of life, is not directly continuous with individuals as individuals. This break in continuity is analogous to that which exists between chemistry and biology. Sociology recognises that there are individual states and predispositions which are taken up and transformed by collective forces. But sociologists who take these well defined individual states as the starting point of their analyses may find, ironically, that these turn out to be consequences of social developments (I: 97–112; II: 125–35). Thirdly, the facts of social morphology have a primary role in sociological explanation since these facts constitute the framework of society's inner environment, and it is to these facts which the origin of all social processes of any significance must be related. In this milieu, constituted by human and physical elements, it is the living human element which is the preponderant factor. The sociological problem then is to discover the properties of this milieu which have the greatest action on social phenomena. Two kinds of characteristics must be taken into account: the volume of a society and its dynamic density measured in terms of the degree of coalescence of its social segments. It is always the action of the 'general social environment' which causes the secondary partial environments to vary. Thus the importance of the concept of the social environment (milieu) is that it permits the sociologist to construct not simply lines of succession but relations of causality. (Comte and Spencer only succeed in establishing empirical successions, believing wrongly that they have established social laws.) The change of function of social practices is made intelligible by this conception, which can now be seen to be connected with the existence of social species (I: 112–21; II: 135–42).

The general character of sociology thus begins to emerge. Whereas for Hobbes the bond between the psychological and the social is synthetic and artificial, and for Spencer is natural and analytic, for Durkheim it is natural and synthetic. Constraint and spontaneity are not oppositions of a Hobbesian or Machiavellian or Spencerian type: tyrannical, artificial or deceptive. They are not in opposition at all: the constraint of the social is naturally spontaneous (I: 121–4; II: 142–4).

Finally, sociological method requires a consideration of proofs. The only adequate method is the comparative method or the method of indirect experimentation. What was called the 'historical method' by Comte has serious weaknesses: it simply expresses an apparent direction of evolution discovered by intuition. J. S. Mill's underlying conception of method must also be rejected because it introduces many unnecessary complications resulting from the idea that the same effect may spring from many different causes: this contradicts the principle of the comparative method. The causal principle of sociology must be: to the same effect there always corresponds the same cause. The method of concomitant variations is thus the instrument of sociology *par excellence*; it establishes, unlike the method of 'residues' or 'agreements' or 'difference', relations of internal causation. But the method is only fruitful if the comparisons are of a series sufficiently continuous and extensive to permit complete analysis. It must not treat single isolated cases. The types of series in comparison can vary from a narrow range formed in one society to the broadest formed by taking societies of different species. A complete analysis therefore must follow the entire development of a social fact through a complete evolutionary series (I: 12–40; II: 147–58).

Three points are made by way of conclusion: first, sociological method must be independent of all philosophy and all practical doctrines. Second, the method is aimed at achieving greater objectivity, and is therefore dominated by the conception that social facts must be treated as things. All the most important consequences of method follow from this. Thirdly, the method is specific to the study of *social* facts. This has the consequence that sociology becomes an autonomous area of study for which a specifically sociological education is required (I: 141–5; II: 159–63).

SOME FIRST OBSERVATIONS AND COMMENTS ON THESE IDEAS

It is now possible to see why the *Rules* is such an explosive document: revolutionary in its ambition to establish a genuine science of social phenomena directly capable of diagnosing social maladies, beyond a purely dialectical or ideological, political diagnosis. It is also, specifically, a critique of the claims of individualism and humanism to be able to identify, other than in a purely ideological manner, the basic structural causes of social pathology; on the other hand, Durkheim's political orientation was not a scientistic illiberalism. Modern individual liberty and equality was to be extended into a liberal socialism: revolutionary communism on the other hand could be identified as a romantic reaction, dangerously uniting elements of violence, utopian social levelling and anarchic individualism. As an intellectual system this false remedy is the inevitable product of over-simple rationalism: the desire for the pure, the avoidance of the inherently complex analytical problems posed by the nature of the social problems of modern societies, analysis based on a single determinant element, and above all, the intervention of the *parti pris* (Durkheim's political vocabulary

PART ONE

specified the modern political problem as a pathological couple: despotism-anarchy).

Durkheim's claim is, then, that the new type of sociologists hold in suspension the loyalty to interest group and adopt the position of the whole – i.e. the social species, not in order to disappear into an ivory tower but to be able to develop a more adequate knowledge of this totality. We might call this Durkheim's *holistic* politics. For this to be effective the sociologist must apply to himself an essentially intellectual and moral self-discipline.

Truth is not produced in relation to the partial desires of particular groups nor can it be defined as a conceptual adequacy to available collections of data as evidence; nor is it the product of rhetorical or dialectical court procedures. Truth is produced in a rational scientific practice dominated by rules of evidence, selection of evidence, classification of forms, methodical comparison, theoretical induction, rules of explanation, rules of proof. The rules of sociological method are, then, none other than the rules for the very production of a true knowledge of social reality. A knowledge which, by its very internal constitution, will imply and begin to specify how society can cure itself.

The project is, thus conceived, extraordinarily ambitious. It is hardly to be wondered at that some have simply baulked at its overwhelming scope. Thus Lévi-Strauss dedicated his work *Structural Anthropology* to the memory of Durkheim as the founder of the *Année Sociologique*, 'that famed workshop where modern anthropology fashioned part of its tools and which we have abandoned, not so much out of disloyalty as out of the sad conviction that the task would prove too much for us' (1972: vi).

3

The Problematic Consistency of Durkheim's 'Official' Method

As regards methods, not one can ever be used that is not provisional, for they change as science progresses. (Durkheim (1901), 1982: 35)

Durkheim never revised his account of sociology's method offered in the *Rules*... and this ... set severe limits on the scope of his methodology and indeed on his understanding of his own post-1895 practice. (S. Lukes, in Durkheim, 1982: 7)

Before examining in detail Durkheim's problems in composing the text of the *Rules* it is essential to examine the evolution of his conception of methodology over the whole of his career. There are two sides to this. One concerns the series of explicit discussions of methodological problems and aims which he wrote at regular intervals; the other concerns his practical efforts of sociological analysis and the discussions of method in these works. One of the persistent criticisms of the *Rules* is that Durkheim himself never applied them, and they are nothing but a flagwaving exercise. In this chapter I will concentrate on the issue of the consistency of the formal declarations of intent which appeared in critical articles and even in public debates. At this stage of the discussion I will simply select a number of considerations of method made at rough intervals: the early works of 1885–8; the works accompanying the *Rules* in the mid-1890s; and selections around 1901, around 1909, and 1915. The aim is to take a cross section through the work of these various periods to reach a view of the kind of method Durkheim was then promoting in them. It is a useful exercise since it is also clear that considerations of method were intimately bound up with Durkheim's claims for the larger role of sociology in the social sciences and beyond.

(i)

The fatal limitations of examining the works of the years around 1895 in isolation are immediately apparent when the essays of the Durkheim's first period of writing are analysed, for when he began teaching sociology and education courses at the University of Bordeaux in 1887–8 he introduced a complex programme of sociological theory and analysis of great originality in which methodological considerations played a key role. He published substantial articles on the teaching of philosophy and a survey of the 'science of morals' in Germany in 1887 which formed the backcloth to the discussions of method in lectures of 1888, and an article on the study of the curious association of birth rates and suicide rates (1888) which inaugurated his keen interest in statistical analysis. In the subsequent three years (1889–91) he published only three short reviews, so the early groups of essays and lectures appear to stand naturally on their own.

These early works, however, contain both a remarkably coherent sociological project and a series of theoretical and procedural principles of great sophistication, not a set of half-formed observations and speculations. In fact even in Durkheim's remarkable first published essay, a review of the work of German sociologist Albert Schaeffle published in 1885, there are striking indications of Durkheim's methodological sureness. And even in this fairly brief article some of the standard themes of Durkheim's position were announced for the first time. He roundly criticised the influence of the Cartesian tradition with its emphasis on an over-simplified rationalism: in France, he proposed, the development of sociology depended on a systematic and determined break with the idea that method in sociology should aim at reducing the complex to the simple (for example, the social to the individual). The introduction and development of biological metaphors were a significant support in assisting this break, but Schaeffle, said Durkheim, stopped short of important conclusions for fear of over-systematising his thought. He failed to provide an adequate conception of social as opposed to psychological phenomena, for he tended to think that social structures were simply vast systems of psychological harmonies held together by individual wills. The time was ripe, claimed Durkheim, for the foundation of sociology as a distinct discipline: 'sociology has now left the heroic age. Its right to exist is no longer contested. Let it be founded and organised and let it outline its programme and specify its method' (Durkheim, 1978: 111).

In this early period this is exactly what Durkheim attempted to do, and more, since he also furnished it with a general theory of social evolution, a conspectus of the range of phenomena falling within its orbit, initial analyses, with a genealogy, and a fundamental politicotherapeutic social rationale. No longer a discipline dependent on outstanding individuals, he judged, sociology had reached the stage of increasing specialisation and internal division. Its branches could be enumerated provisionally as concerning a) collective ideas and sentiments (legends, religious traditions, language, etc.); b) morality which has general social sanctions attached to it; c) a specific group of moral norms which are obligatory and sanctioned by socially authorised agents; d) economic phenomena. Two more areas are indicated as potential branches for sociological study but as yet remain unfounded: e) military and f) diplomatic phenomena. All of these are social facts and could be studied through the comparative method. More than this, their structures could be divided into the terrains of structure and function, morphology and physiology, bearing in mind both that in the higher organisms there need be no one-to-one relation of structure and function and no absolute division between the two, since structure is function consolidated. Function, the active moment, is by implication fundamental.

An outline of his course on the sociology of the family (published in 1888) sketched out the theoretical and methodological elements of the larger programme which he had covered in the previous year: 'before going ahead we had to know what bonds unite men to one another or, in other words, what determines the formation of social aggregates' (Durkheim, 1978: 205). The whole of the first year of the course (1887–8) seems to have been an initial exploration of the theme, later elaborated at length in the *Division*, the movement, caused by the 'simultaneous increase of the volume and density of societies', in social evolution from forms dominated by mechanical to those dominated by organic solidarity (1978: 205–6). Durkheim called this a course on the 'general forms of sociability and their laws' (1978: 207), a course necessarily prior to undertaking specialised studies such as an investigation into the sociology of the family. This latter study was then discussed in terms of what Durkheim considered the ideal programme of investigation (1978: 207–10), and then what in fact could be done – 'less rigorous and less precise' but it could still yield 'important results' (1978: 211). This kind of balance sheet, with its calculation, suspension, setting out of alternative courses of action, is characteristic: in this case, Durkheim argues that a reliable knowledge of the various types of families, the empirical basis of such a study, was simply not available: a more preliminary groundwork had to be laid – the attempt to formulate an evolutionary classification, and an initial functional comparison of the types established (1978: 211).

Along with this programmatic statement, Durkheim also published in that year a study of 'moral statistics' relating birth rates and suicide rates. Here the question revolved around the problem of trying to identify conditions of social health and pathology. In this project he began to establish a statistical correlation between an abnormally high birth rate and a rising suicide rate, as well as one between an abnormally low birth rate and a rising suicide rate. A normal rate, he argued, was one which fell between certain stable limits beyond which it would become pathological. If in the analysis of birth and suicide rates abnormalities were connected with some unknown cause, this was not to be found among the facts of individual biology, or race, but in a truly social determinant. In order to reach an understanding of this cause it would be necessary to analyse the relations in the domestic milieu which might provide protection against suicide tendencies. It was known, for example, that married were more protected than unmarried people, and that suicide rates were higher where divorce was more common. He concluded by suggesting that when the birth rate declines the associated increase in suicides could be related in part to a regression in domestic moral relations (Durkheim, 1975a, ii, 235).

Here, evidently, are some of the elements which have given Durkheim a reputation for positivism (emphasis on classification and statistical correlation, etc.), but also for overactive theoretical speculation and even traces of mysticism (the idea that there are moral causes), but also, further, for inconsistency (since he has also suggested that social evolution is determined by factors such as social volume and density, i.e. material and moral forces). I will return to discuss these issues in a later chapter. It is also important to notice at this point the structure of the programme and its methodological flexibility. In his 1888 lecture introducing the sociological study of the family, he suggested that classification, though important, is only a stage in the analytic process; beyond that comes the essential moment of experimentation. An experiment cannot be defined as the simple production of artificial relations, he said, but as the attempt to vary elements and their relationships in order to discover invariant connections. Although sociologists cannot manipulate their material as is possible in other disciplines, such experiments can be made indirectly, by examining and comparing naturally produced combinations (Durkheim, 1978: 210). This implies that sociology must use the inductive method. Scientific sociology would then require the establishment of proofs and to follow these with secondary verifications where possible. The objective is to reach a position where the formulation of true socio-logical laws becomes a real possibility.

The order of discussion of the lecture is interesting, for after out-lining the nature of the general forms of solidarity, and the conception of indirect experimentation, he then suggested that the sociologist must also be aware of the nature of the raw materials of his inves-tigations which are less than objective, indeed the sociologist should 'discard' all subjective narrative accounts of family life. It is only at this point in the exposition that he raised the question which opens the *Rules,* of what kind of criterion the sociologist should use in identifying the range of facts which fall within his terrain. Impression-istic accounts may well focus on idiosyncratic features of a particular culture. What is essential is that sociology identifies correctly: 'a way of acting not only habitual but obligatory for all members of a society' (1978: 214).

The existence in any society of a social sanction used to maintain a norm indicates that the practice is more than a habit or an idiosyncrasy, it is a phenomenon of a quite different order. It indicates that there has been produced phenomena acting with genuine necessity 'analogous to those studied in the natural sciences'. But in selecting these for study there is a cost, for any such selection concentrates analysis exclusively on those customs and practices which have become consolidated in this way, with the disadvantage that the more fluid currents in the life of society, some of which may be of great importance, will not have been taken into account. However, it may be possible to study more fleeting currents through statistical means, already developed in demography for instance.

In order that such a sociology succeed it must refuse all pressures which lead to the reduction of social facts to individual causes, or to the evasion of social analysis because the object is believed to be too complex. It must also adopt an untroubled frame of mind, the specific mental attitude of 'perfect serenity' in these studies: 'we must rid our minds of prejudices, both optimistic and pessimistic' (1978: 219). It is necessary to avoid all a priori value considerations in the analysis, since ideas of absolute superiority and inferiority of social types have not the slightest scientific value. This is not to say that Durkheim wanted at this stage to separate fact and value, for the Opening Lecture was concluded by specifying the basic problem of modern societies as 'a weakness of the collective spirit' (1978: 69), the solution to which sociology might contribute.

Whatever the merit or originality of these ideas, Durkheim also wanted to make it clear that they had not 'miraculously appeared out of nowhere one sunny day' (1978: 61), for they were part of a tradition: they had historical antecedents and had close neighbours and allies. Briefly, the lineage which Durkheim outlined began in antiquity with Aristotle, the first to treat society as a natural phenomenon, and in modern times with Montesquieu and Condorcet. But the full consequences of treating society as a natural fact were not drawn by any of these writers; even the political economists who first sought the nature of social laws saw only the individual as real, a crucial obstacle to the development of social science. It was Comte, immersed in the theories of natural and biological sciences and their methodologies, who founded sociology definitively, for sociology begins only when society is treated as an irreducibly complex object and its methods aligned with those of the other sciences. The difficulty with Comte's system was that its object, society, though isolated as a natural fact, was still conceived ideologically, as the collective phenomenon 'humanity'. Assumptions of this kind inevitably produced a conception of social evolution as a simple unilinear development. His sociology, at bottom, only envisaged the existence of one social type through history. He therefore revived, mistakenly, Pascal's image of humanity as a single man who had lived throughout all past epochs. But the fact that he also thought sociology required a special method, distinct from other scientific methods, seemed to indicate an awareness that the new science was not yet satisfactorily integrated with the other sciences he had identified.

In fact it was only with the work of the English sociologist Herbert Spencer that the integration of sociology with the other sciences was satisfactorily achieved, Durkheim suggests, through the systematic application of the evolutionist idea to social phenomena. Spencer was able to define the object of sociology with far more precision, and to begin the work of classification of social types. But there were serious problems arising from the way that the evolutionary principle was applied. He sought to prove that social development occurred in conformity with the general law of evolution rather than to discover the existence of the law of evolution in societies. His analyses really only amounted to providing illustrations of an already preconceived general plan of social evolution: inevitably he rediscovers everywhere the same fundamental law.

Positive method was also applied to social subjects by a wide range of scholars in parallel with Spencer's efforts. Durkheim mentions Espinas and Schaeffle as providing materials for sociology; Ihering and Post for work in positive theory of law and Wagner and Schmoller for political economy. In developing links with these neighbouring disciplines, he suggests, sociology 'lost that erstwhile air of sudden improvisation' (Durkheim, 1978: 61).

(ii)

I have, of course, already presented the *Rules* itself in an earlier chapter, but it is important to recognise that there are other important methodological discussions in the texts of the years 1892–5. These bear witness to the success of a large number of initial investigations discussed in lecture courses following the proclamation of the programme of 1888, with its distinctive methodological orientation. These applications were itemised by Durkheim in the lectures on socialism given in 1895–6, as studies of suicide, the family, marriage, punishment, responsibility, and religion (Durkheim, 1960a: 44). Durkheim's lectures had also covered issues in moral and intellectual education, psychology applied to education, and from 1893 he had taught classes for the *agregation* in philosophy. He had also published in 1892 his secondary thesis concerning the originality of Montesquieu's contribution to method in the social sciences. He thus had maintained a broad contact with a large number of disciplines as well as developing new lines. In 1895 he also wrote a synoptic report on the state of French sociology to an Italian journal which provided his project with a detailed account of friends and enemies closer to home than any account of sociology's genealogy or rules of method could do directly.

This report identified three main groupings, represented by the work of three individuals: Letourneau's, Tarde's, and his own. The first was anthropological in orientation, based on a grouping around the Société d'Anthropologie de Paris founded by Broca in 1859. Letourneau's contribution was a 'vast enterprise' involving an attempt to map out the main features of social evolution in the principal social institutions. While saluting its grandeur, Durkheim suggested the methodological orientation was uncritical and ideological (Marxist): its conclusions were always contained in its assumptions. It was a reductionism of a Marxist type in which humanity could, if only it would realise it, throw off its chains and return to a state of primitive simplicity (communism). Marxism in this guise, he concluded, is a variation on the theme of revolutionary individualism. The second group in France, according to Durkheim, was associated with the journal *Archive d'Anthropologie Criminelle*, whose principal writers were Lacassagne and Tarde. The work of the latter was interesting since it contained criticisms of analyses which reduced social to physical phenomena, but the conception of society itself seemed flawed by philosophical assumptions concerning the nature of individuals. The basic proposition, that social facts were produced by individual imitation, was developed only by assertion and dialectical argument, not by any effort at providing a rigorous proof. Undoubtedly, said Durkheim, Tarde attacked assumptions of a priorism and teleological argument, but the suggestion that social development occurred randomly and by chance introduced irrationalist assumptions. The way of posing the problem itself failed to specify methodological checks to the speculations developed. In introducing the third group of writers, which he located in the universities in France, he attacked once again the ingrained rationalism found in France which sought clarity through simplification and mathematisation. It was necessary to enlarge the scope of the application of rationalism far beyond its Cartesian limits for social science to become a possibility. This modification may not be possible, he noted, in other national cultures where there was opposition to the search for social laws, even though it might be acknowledged that social trends and regularities exist. Sociology could only develop where two conditions were met. One current deflects the sociologist from being satisfied with simplistic conceptions, the other supports the application of scientific method with the faith that such an application would not be lost in an object that is without structure or is too obscure or complex to be analysed. It was 'in France that one finds the conditions most favourable to the progress of sociology' (Durkheim, 1975a,i: 107), he concluded.

He then concluded the survey with an outline of his own contribution, the specificity of which he claimed attempted to found itself on an 'objective method' and tried to establish the criterion of objectivity in its definition of its object of study. The principal obstacle to this step was the old materialist argument, this time presented under the guise of spiritualism, which holds that social phenomena were essentially different from physical ones and thus could not be treated by the scientific method. It was therefore essential to insist again that social facts must be defined through the characteristic 'imperative force' they exercise over the will of the individual. Realities cannot be forged directly in relation to the demands of individual pleasure or imagination, indeed they must be conceived as being 'imposed' on the individual. Thus a social fact must be defined as any way of thinking, acting or feeling to which we are obliged to conform (1975a:i, 102).

Much of this review, then, is taken up with criticisms of failures and obstacles, an identification of what Durkheim's sociology sought to combat; it reiterates the basic themes of objectivity and complexity. These were also presented in Durkheim's essay on Montesquieu of 1892, where other important themes concerning the conditions necessary for the emergence of sociology proper (that society be treated as a natural object) and for the classification of social types (that political form not be the basis of classification), etc., were argued. Here two elements can be emphasised, remarks on pathology and on comparisons – both areas where, Durkheim argued, Montesquieu could be criticised. First, Montesquieu, following Aristotle, thought that what was diseased was somehow unnatural. This introduced an element of contingency into the analysis, for it connected the normal and the perfect, and as societies rarely seemed perfect the causes of imperfection seemed accidental, unrelated to the types of cause operative on the normal condition. But, Durkheim suggests, this is a crucial error, 'disease no less than health is inherent in the nature of living things' (Durkheim, 1965: 46). Secondly, because Montesquieu thought of societies as having forms that were only rarely dependent on one another, there was no sense of the progression of social evolution in his work and thus neither an attempt to outline a social series, nor to identify social conflicts which inevitably emerge as societies change (1965: 59).

The major writings on method in this period, however, were the Introduction to the *Division* of 1893, and the *Rules* of 1894, to which I will return in a later chapter.

PART ONE

(iii)

If we turn to the group of articles and essays of the years around 1900 there are also a large number of significant texts to consider, and, if we add to these some of the methodological writings of the newly established Durkheimian *Année* school of sociology, it is possible to see a consolidation of positions on a number of these problems. Marcel Mauss later, around 1930, claimed that a second book on method after the *Rules* had been projected at this stage, to be jointly authored by Durkheim, Mauss and Fauconnet, the main sections of which, however, he says were published independently. The main essays are Durkheim's essays 'Sociology in France in the Nineteenth Century' (1900); 'Sociology and its Scientific Field' (1900); 'On the Objective Method in Sociology' (1901, the second Preface to the *Rules*); 'Sociology' (Fauconnet and Mauss, 1901); and 'Sociology and Social Sciences' (Durkheim and Fauconnet, 1903).

These works do in fact have great collective coherence. The second (1901) Preface is a reply to criticisms of the first edition of the *Rules*. Though published as a separate article, 'Sociology in France' is a discussion of the main periods of sociology in France from Saint Simon. Fauconnet and Mauss's essay attempts to restate the object, method and main divisions of sociology and allied to this essay is the statement by Durkheim of the 'Scientific Field' of sociology (which is also a reply to objections by Simmel). The final piece is a comprehensive survey of the development of the 'sociological idea' at work in various fields of specialised research which might profit from recognising this common orientation and benefit from mutual contact. It might also be suggested indeed that there are other works which might be considered here: the discussion of the difference between individual and collective representations (1898), the large numbers of reviews on methodological problems written for the *Année* which appeared annually between 1898–1907. Here, however, the discussion will focus on the definitions of object and methods of sociology itself, as discussed in Durkheim's essay on sociology's scientific domain, his second preface to the *Rules* and Fauconnet and Mauss's essay on sociology.

The preface to the second edition (1901) of the *Rules* was also published separately with the title 'On the Objective Method in Sociology'. It sought to reply to criticisms on three scores: his proposition that social facts should be treated as things, that social facts can be viewed as external to the individual, and his definition of the social fact itself. In replying to his critics Durkheim's central assertion was that what was essential to his position were not rules concerning classification of social types, or for distinguishing between normal and pathological forms, etc.; these are secondary issues, but the connection between objectivity, externality and the conception of a truly sociological domain.

He reiterated, firstly, the position that social phenomena must be treated as things. In suggesting such a position it was not intended to indicate that the nature of these objects were material or physical. All that was suggested was that the fundamental character of a thing be understood as something which had inherent resistance to pure human desire or will. Perhaps, he says, mathematical objects do not have such resistance and this would have to be reflected upon, but for those disciplines which did have as their aim the study of objects in the world of nature, these objects cannot be known through the method of introspection. The advances in psychology had shown the effectiveness of avoiding purely introspectionist techniques.

Secondly, the idea that social phenomena are external to individuals had been hotly disputed. Yet the argument in the *Rules* amounted to saying that society is an emergent property, a *sui generis* reality. Durkheim here drew on his important paper, published in 1898, on 'Individual and Collective Representations'. The relevant argument was presented at much greater length and depth in that paper which also, incidentally, indicated some of Durkheim's developing ideas on the conception of social facts. It seems appropriate here to make a slight digression in order to consider the paper.

Durkheim's (1898) paper takes up a new line of approach to the question of the relative autonomy of the social domain. Instead of basing himself on an analogy of the properties which are emergent between chemical and biological phenomena he now turned to the emergent properties of the distinctively psychological compared with the biological. This whole essay underlines the great interest Durkheim took in the debates and developments in psychology in the 1890s; indeed that he taught courses in psychology at Bordeaux is often forgotten or overlooked. Far from adopting 'crude' and 'naive' views on the nature of the individual, Durkheim's position was abreast of the major developments at the decisive moment of the formation of modern psychology. He did not, however, attempt to derive a new sociology out of psychology, but tried to take the new principles whereby psychological phenomena had been identified and use them for similar sociological reasoning. Durkheim notes, with interest, that the biological reductionists in psychology found it difficult to respond adequately to those like Janet who proposed the thesis that the *sui generis* character of individual representations were external to the biological substratum which carried them. Durkheim discussed the problem of memory and tackled the apparent logical problem of the existence of forms of consciousness in the individual of which the individual was not at all aware, so-called unconscious phenomena. Durkheim examined the evidence of hypnosis and other experimental evidence and suggested that the reality of the unconscious could not be denied. Perhaps the best way to conceive it, he suggested, is in terms of primary and secondary sites of consciousness. The unconscious would then lie in those sites which were beyond the central apparatus of the ego (Durkheim, 1953: 22–3).

In order to make these developments, he argued, psychology had no recourse at all to introspection. 'Science goes from without, from the external and immediately sensible manifestations, to the interior characteristics.' And 'If, then, we are forced to say that certain phenomena can only be caused by representations, that these representations are the outward signs of representational life, and if, on the other hand, the subject in whom these representations appear is ignorant of them, we shall say that unconscious states exist' (1953: 19–20). This idea is then used, by Durkheim, for immediate reflection on the way that collective representations should be approached. The substratum is, of course, the individual. Analytically, social phenomena must be thought of as exterior to the substratum. Thus it is necessary to explain this new emergent property, the social, not by reference to the individual, the simple (materialist metaphysical reduction), or the simple by the complex (idealist metaphysics), but the complex by the complex, which is simply scientific method applied to this natural emergent reality (1953: 29).

Turning to the *sui generis* nature of collective representations, he suggested that once a number of them had been formed they develop their own partial autonomy, they form new syntheses 'which are determined by their natural affinities and not by the condition of their matrix ... they are caused by other collective representations and not by this or that characteristic of the social structure' (1953: 31). The religious beliefs of Greece and Rome cannot be explained directly by the morphology of those societies. On the other hand, to suggest that there are extra-social forces at work is completely illusory. What was present here, he argued, was a complex relation of primary and derived phenomena: and perhaps, he suggested, a special branch of sociology itself should be produced to attempt to analyse such secondary formations.

The conception of the social fact developed here was consistent with the earlier one where obligation was given as 'the proof that these ways of acting and thinking are not the work of the individual'; this characteristic, he stressed once more, was presented solely as a convenient external sign of the existence of the social phenomenon, not in any way a 'summary explanation' of it.

It is this point which is taken up directly in 1901 if we return now to the Second Preface to the *Rules*. There Durkheim added that the social fact could also be thought of as presenting, perhaps, the opposite characteristic to obligation, duty and coercion, that of the desirable and the good. This second characteristic is, he noted, something that seems 'more internal and intimate' than duty. It is also something that makes the social fact appear less tangible and difficult to perceive. It was, however, in no sense intended, in the *Rules*, to deny the existence of this characteristic. It is a complete misunderstanding to attribute to the argument in the *Rules* any attempt to *explain* social facts by reference to constraint, or to develop through this line of inquiry any philosophical idea of social reality as in itself constraining. The rules were introduced in order to provide only an initial, rational definition of the nature of the external signature of social phenomena themselves. The social fact, however, can and will be characterised in many different ways. It is even possible to apply more than one at the same time. But this choice is a question of tactics.

Many other definitions of the social fact have been proffered: the idea, for example, that the social fact must be conceived as 'all that is produced in and by society'. But it is clear this is not completely adequate. Durkheim does not identify the source of this idea in the Second Preface, but he had already discussed it at some length in an essay of 1900 on 'Sociology and its Scientific Domain'. We can turn to this as a second digression fron the 1901 Preface. Durkheim developed the idea that sociology has its specific terrain in a critique of the ideas of the influential German sociologist, Georg Simmel. The idea that the objects of sociology are the forms of group association, rather than any specific content of social action, a mode, that is, rather than a substance of interaction, was criticised as one-sided and metaphysical. Durkheim suggested that it was important to recognise two sides of

sociology, morphology and physiology. The external form of morphology includes (i) the territorial, the relation between nations, the
form of frontiers, etc., (ii) the structure of populations, the formation
of cities, towns, villages, habitations, etc., (iii) the use of soils, systems
of communication, markets, etc. All these are the results of active
social forces and in turn act as social forces. The Comtean idea, he
noted, that this can be grasped only in a pure social statics is quite
wrong, such structures are encountered in their becoming, they are
forms of life consolidated. On the other hand, to call it simply a form
as does Simmel is to adopt a metaphor in place of a concept.

The other side of sociology is the study of function (physiology).
These too are *sui generis* phenomena, and are not revealed by 'intrinsic'
characteristics. If they are conceived as social facts this does not imply
violence or indoctrination for 'normally, a moral authority invests all
the products of its activity and bends our spirits and wills' (Durkheim,
1962: 365). Out of these phenomena can be selected for study a special
group which include sanctioned acts, and these form a field of sociological objects which are 'different from all other forms of actions and
ideas' (1962: 366). There is a range of other social phenomena beyond
this category, including language, traditions, fashions, even the levels
of technical development which are 'consecrated' and resist alteration
or subversion. The active force in the heart of the moral milieu
'consists in that prestige *sui generis* which is the privilege of social
facts' (1962: 367).

The discussion then moves to the problem of 'sociological explanation'. It recapitulates sections of the *Rules* but ends with the observation that there are three kinds (*cadres*) of sociological explanation:
1. the connection of one collective representation to another (example:
penal law and private vengeance); 2. the connection of a collective
representation to a fact of social structure (for example, right of
property with the formation of towns); 3. connection of facts of social
structure with determined collective representations (for example,
certain myths and the movement of migration of the Jews, etc.). These
explanations may move in circles which follow causal realities in
themselves. The consideration of 'method of sociology', examines the
problems of definition, observation of facts, systematisation of facts,
and the scientific character of sociological hypotheses. The essay suggested that no effective method can be established abstractly, and that
what is presented is in effect 'a number of scientific procedures already
sanctioned by usage' (in Mauss, 1968–9, Vol. 3: 164). As this section

is so important as a secondary clarification of Durkheimian pı.
and as it is not available in English tradition, it is worth preseı.
the ideas in some detail.

Fauconnet and Mauss suggest that definition is a decisive methodological element: it organises the field, it prevents communication at
cross purposes, prevents conceptual confusions. On the other hand,
its object is not to establish phenomenal essences, but a provisional
clarification by the application of rational principles to the field presented to us by society itself. Such definitions are constructs but not
constructs *a priori*. They are a résumé of a first rapid review of
the facts, constructed with the aim of substituting initial rational
classification in place of those found already to hand in society. These
definitions, also, establish a certain set of obligations on the sociologist
to adopt a certain type of intellectual rigour and discipline. With good
initial definitions, which may cut across conventional boundaries,
sociologists may find that they have to search anew for facts which
not only might positively support a theory, but also for those which,
because the logic of definition suggests it should be included, may
violently disturb preconceptions.

If Durkheim sought here to retain the balance between morphology
and physiology he was concerned, to return again to the 1901 Preface,
to criticise the notion that he had suggested social facts work through
sheer physical necessity. Obviously the action of sheer natural necessity
can be considered a constraint on action, but it is not constraint of a
social kind. It is not from the 'unyieldingness of certain patterns of
molecules' that social facts constrain, but from the prestige which they
possess. Indeed the social fact seems to have the character of all
institutions, moral authority and intellectual and this term may be
taken, 'provided one extends a little its normal meaning' (Durkheim,
1982: 45), to designate the object of sociology: 'all beliefs and modes
of conduct instituted by the collectivity'.

This new formulation was taken from a complementary essay by
Fauconnet and Mauss called 'Sociology'. This work which may even
have had Durkheim's cooperation, is an attempt to give a brief outline
of Durkheimian sociology, its object and method. Far from being a
pallid paraphrase of the *Rules* the essay has its own distinctive character and individuality. It is an interesting restatement of the principles
in the *Rules*. One of its most striking features is its organisation, which
suggests something of a fundamental reassessment of categories. It
begins with a section called 'The Object of Sociology', which has a

outlining a terrain of natural social facts, then a phenomena'. The social order is a *sui generis* , the economic life of modern societies, language, nd domestic relations, religion, intellectual and istoms, mores, superstitions, etc., are all dependent of the social group in which they are found. In this na there are some social facts which appear to be sanctioned anu a.ᴄ obligatory. But there are others where the individual appears to be not only beyond obligation, but where he is almost beyond the action of social forces. One way of approaching the facts at work here is to examine them as structures which the individual already finds in existence and which are transmitted from generation to generation, by education, and socialisation. If these structures are called 'institutions' it has to be stressed that they are far from being static entities but are constantly in the process of formation and transformation. This is not a definitive definition, because it leaves to one side, provisionally, those collectivities which are without institutional forms, such as crowds.

If the process of definition rests on a first review of facts, a kind of provisional observation, it is then necessary to pass to methodical observation. Like other disciplines, sociology does not narrate, or simply describe, it does not simply 'photograph' brute facts. In reality, it constitutes them, it abstracts. In studying them it adopts appropriate techniques, historical, documentary, statistical, etc. Critical work on these facts then becomes essential. For example, official statistics are often based on national legal categories which severely influence the degree to which they can be compared between nations. On the other hand sociological comparisons only become possible between cultures on the basis of critical analysis of historical and social accounts: the sociologist does not have to possess infinite capacities, only a demand for exact and reliable material. A social fact thus described ceases to belong to a particular time or place. It is placed, by the force of scientific observation, outside of time or space.

The facts thus produced must be placed in a rational system. Generally, it is impossible to find immediate causal relations, special methodological procedures have to be employed. These have to be specific forms of comparison, working either through the use of statistics or through the treatment of social evolution as a natural experimental laboratory. The aim should not be endless accumulation of materials, but the formulation of elementary, but 'severe', comparisons. This can be achieved in three stages: 1. ordering of facts, only facts of the same order must be used; 2. facts must be placed in strictly defined series of increasing or decreasing complexity; 3. comparisons between the series so constructed that they can be used as a basis to form hypotheses.

The hypotheses which are produced in these circumstances are obviously not absolute, but they do have a strictly scientific character. First, they are explanations of a truly structural type. They also indicate necessary connections which allow through induction the formulation of certain predictions. Thirdly and most important they are open to rational criticism and verification. 'Hypothesis becomes an element of precise discussion; one can contest, rectify method, initial definition, facts, established comparisons' and, in these new conditions, science can make progress (Mauss, 1968-9, Vol. 3: 173).

A final major heading of their essay deals with 'Divisions of Sociology'. Other social sciences seem to exist, they argue, alongside sociology, and in recent years, they say, there has been a remarkable rapprochement of these disciplines with the idea of sociology. The introduction of sociological method will begin to alter the relations between these disciplines and a more rational division between them will be possible. But the 'special disciplines' will then be complemented by a new general sociology which will study the unity of all social phenomena.

This last theme was developed at length in a related paper by Durkheim and Fauconnet published in 1903, 'Sociology and Social Sciences'. It is a wide ranging and ambitious attempt to survey the fields which have begun to recognise the significance of the 'sociological idea'. It is focussed, squarely, on the problem that sociology itself, and particularly Durkheimian sociology, is based on the assertion that there is a specific domain of sociological objects, while at the same time many distinct social sciences already exist which partly cut across that territory. The paper argues that 'sociology is and can only be the system, the corpus, of the social sciences' and that the social sciences and their methods are the process of radical reorganisation (Durkheim, 1982: 175). Other previous approaches to this problem are inadequate: Comte's synthetic philosophy is philosophical not sociological; Spencer's opposition of specialism and unification is contradictory: Mill's ruling 'general science' which provides the specialisms with t⌙ postulates is untenable, as is Giddings' idea that general studies the indeterminate, or Simmel's idea that it studi forms. What is required is, in the first place, a greater degree of co-operation. Comte's vision may, in some form, then be realised as the co-operation develops. The unity of the social sciences can 'only have as its mechanism a body of distinct but solidly linked sciences' and, from the new relationships established, will grow new common doctrines which could become the subject of a rejuvenated social philosophy.

Finally, one other essay, by Durkheim himself, selected from this period, attempts to survey the achievements of French sociology in the nineteenth century (1900). Sociology, he declared, was born in France and is a specifically French product. Before he introduced his own contributions to this tradition, Durkheim noted the existence of three distinct periods: a first period of effervescence with the work of Saint Simon, Fourier and Comte, coming to an end around 1848; a period of great stagnation until 1870; then a second effervescence. These periods must be related to profound causes, he suggested, but mused that it is difficult to see how intellectual work could be so profoundly affected, say, by political conditions alone. In recent years, he argued, the social sciences entered the era of specialisation. The result was that, while sociology remained too general, the special disciplines lacked analytic method. 'The most urgent reform was therefore to make the sociological idea come down into these special techniques, and by that very fact to transform them, truly making of them social sciences' (Durkheim, 1973a: 15–16). It was in response to this situation, he said, that the *Rules* were written. There are two characteristics to the method: it is based on the idea that there is a specific realm of social facts, and secondly, that this method is naturalistic and opposes the anthropocentric point of view. The effervescence of French sociology, he claimed, is due to two basic causes: the marked weakening of traditionalism in France, and the survival of a specific form of rationalism in France. It is in France, specifically, that people have most taken up the challenge of the analysis of social structure in the belief of discovering the laws of its inner nature. The main problem in France, however, is that simple Cartesian rationalism in its unreformed mode remains an obstacle to sociology. Sociology depends on the development of complex rationalism.

(iv)

The period around 1909 was again marked by popularisations of method. The main one was again also called 'Sociology and Social Sciences' (1909). It is divided into three components. The first, another genealogy of the formation of sociology, continues the theme that sociology is the application of the principle of determinism to the new object – society. The second looks at the individual social sciences which are divided between morphological sciences (e.g. political geography) and those of physiology (which includes the study of religion, morality, law, economy as its main branches, and the study of languages and aesthetics as new immature ones). There is also, now, a 'general sociology' which studies the social fact *in abstracto* and asks whether there are general social laws. The third part examines 'the sociological method', which Durkheim presents as the method of comparative history. An institution is a complex reality made up of parts, but these are difficult to determine for there may be no natural visible demarcation line which separates them out. Institutions form gradually ' piece by piece', so the parts may have accumulated over time. An historical study will reveal how these pieces were assembled; history, in fact, can operate for the investigator a natural process of association and disassociation. A study of kinship, for example, shows that what appears simple has a complex historical process of formation. This method alone permits the formulation of explanations which account for the elements which occur in the formative process. Causal explanation must then trace the fact back to its moment of appearance, for only in this way is it possible to identify the way in which the cause produced its effect: it is necessary in other words to 'observe it at the very moment when it was born and to be present at its genesis' (Durkheim, 1978: 84). Sociology thus conceived has a special link with history, but, whereas the work of the historian concerns specific societies, that of the sociologist is comparative and experimental. So, there is 'only one way' to determine a causal connection to investigate by observing variations whether the appearance, or absence, of two or more facts reveal a dependence or not. There are other cases where a resort to the analysis of statistics is profitable, such as the frequency of homicide, marriages, divorces, wages, rents, interest rates, etc. The sociologist must also adopt a certain attitude to the phenomena being studied, consciously adopting the point of view of the scientist, and must 'begin by making a *tabula rasa* of the notions' he or she has of the reality to be studied. The sociologist must 'set aside', 'forget' the

PART ONE

everyday notions of these objects. The task is to begin to discover the
nature of these phenomena, and this always involves the displacement
of 'ready-made and deceptive truisms' (1978: 87).

Durkheim also published an essay on the relation between 'the
sociology of religion and the theory of knowledge' in 1909, which
indicated his conception at this time of the relation between sociology
and psychology on the one hand and sociology and philosophy on the
other. It contains some important observations on misconceptions of
the sociological project.

First, far from attempting to set up a sociology which is interested
only in the 'external' forms of institutions, 'we deem that the sociologist
will not have completely accomplished his mission so long as he has
not penetrated the inmost depth of individuals, in order to relate their
psychological condition' to institutions (Durkheim, 1982: 236). The
strategy, however, involves making an understanding of the nature of
humankind a goal, not a point of departure. 'Far from sociology, so
conceived, being a stranger to psychology, it arrives itself at a
psychology, but one far more concrete and complex...' (1982: 237).

Secondly, he suggested, while there is no hostility to philosophy, as
such, there is no sympathy for a narrowly conceived empiricism. On
the contrary, sociology aims to reinvigorate theoretical philosophy.
But philosophy must either work on the materials provided by the
sciences or on literature. But as the sciences become more specialised,
philosophy it seems would have to develop an encyclopaedic knowledge in order to make progress. Sociology represents a different possibility because it is an integrative discipline: it is related to an object
collective representations which itself is synthetic, 'it is the collective
consciousness which is the true microcosm' of society (1982: 238): and
further, amongst these representations, social categories are preponderant. They are dominant because they condense within them the
whole of the civilisations of which they are the product. In order to
study categories it is important to reject the above all 'dialectical and
ideological method' of the Kantians. 'If the categories are the net result
of history and collective action, if their genesis is one in which each
individual has only an infinitesimal share and which has even occurred
almost beyond his own field of action, we must ... if we seek to
philosophise about things rather than words, begin by confronting
these categories as if faced with unknown realities whose nature,
causes and functions have to be determined...' (1982: 239).

(v)

A final period can be established around the brief article 'Sociology' that Durkheim wrote in 1915. Durkheim in this final period again traced the history of the formation of sociology from Montesquieu and Condorcet, Saint Simon to Comte. Little remains, he noted, of Comte's doctrine which now had historical interest only. After the period of stagnation in mid-century, sociology again began to flourish. First the project was general. With the emergence of Durkheim's own work it has entered into the 'age of specialisation'. Three groups of social facts had been studied: religious, moral/legal, and economic. Each of these has again been broken down into sub-specialisations, in the work of Hubert and Mauss, Bouglé, Simiand, Halbwachs, and Lévy-Bruhl. Many of the topic areas had long made their public appearance and what was needed was an effort to bring them into contact and to review their interrelationships. In order to make this rapprochement effective the *Année Sociologique* was established in 1896, in a tradition fundamentally inspired by Comte. Durkheim then reviewed again the work of Tarde, and other groups of secondary authors (Letourneau, Dumont, Coste, etc). Finally, he noted that 'sociology could have been born and developed only where the two conditions ... existed in combination: first traditionalism had to have lost its domain ... second, a veritable faith in the power of reason to dare to undertake the translation of the most complex and unstable of realities into definite terms was necessary' (Durkheim *et al.*, 1960a: 383). France possessed that combination, and being now aware of the excessive and dangerous simplicism of Cartesian thought would move to a higher form of rationalism.

If we turn to Durkheim's last project, the project on *Ethics* he was beginning to put together in 1917, there are again some interesting methodological comments, as Durkheim attempted to draft an introductory statement. In fact there are two remaining drafts. The shorter one, apparently more sketchy, specifies that the sociologist should attempt to avoid, where possible, the errors of the moralists and the psychologists. The former, he thought, attempt to analyse morality but always substitute an already available idea from which analysis deduces moral forms. The latter try to establish the nature of human psychology in general and then deduce from this the ways in which morals appear in history. Both are erroneous, and so, in order to avoid these mistakes, a controlling method has to be employed. He wrote:

41

For the scientist there is no reality which is self-evident; there is none which in the initial stages of research is not and must not be treated as an unknown quantity. In order to discover its nature, we must first make use of the external signs which are its most obvious manifestations. We then substitute others in place of these external and perceptible signs as our research progresses. But it is only when we have gone beyond the realm of sensory appearances that it is possible to discover the profound characteristics of the thing itself, those which comprise its essence, in so far as that word can be used in scientific terminology. (Durkheim, 1978: 266–7)

Science proceeds, then, by treating morality as a natural phenomenon which should be approached through its external characteristics. These are classified, arranged into types, their place in 'the totality of other phenomena' determined and their causes analysed (1978: 199).

4

Variations of Method in Durkheim's Sociological Analyses

It is in the application that a method must be judged. (Durkheim (1907) 1980: 138)

Few scholars have recognised that Durkheim's avowed methodological ideal in the *Rules* only slightly resembles his actual method, (E. Wallwork, 1972: 6–7)

After this account of Durkheim's descriptions of his method, I now want to discuss some specific features of selected works, looking especially at their methodological particularities.

DIVISION

The expositional logic of the *Division* hinges crucially on propositions in its first chapter, one of the most fiercely militant epistemological opening chapters of any major work of sociology. With dramatic and relentless logic Durkheim shows that the emergence of division of labour cannot be explained through appeal to human desire or need, i.e., teleologically, for these are themselves bound up with the changes which have to be accounted for, and thus have themselves to be explained. If the real object of study is moral conscience itself it is necessary to find a way of investigating it through an intermediary, an effect. This can be the complex connection of crime and punishment. From the existence of two types of sanction, which relate to two types of law, two types of social structure can be deduced. One of these is more primitive, the other resting on the division of labour develops progressively and is a derived phenomenon. In order to analyse this process it is necessary to identify the efficient causes and the functions of the division of labour. If this is done, it becomes clear that the former is not the cause of the latter, and that the functions of the latter do not cause it to come into existence. The causes must be sought elsewhere.

It can be seen that much of this logic is completely independent of the evidence analysed; indeed at this point very little evidence has been analysed. The central problems in the exposition centre on the problem of the definition of crime itself, the main issue of Chapter Two, and the purely theoretical problem of the unity of the crime–punishment complex. The force of Durkheim's argument hinges on being able to substantiate the definition of crime as any act which infringes the social conscience and which receives a response in the form of a sanction from society. Two problems can be noted here. The first is the criticism of Garafalo's definition of crime, which draws a methodological rule (repeated in the *Rules*), the second is the problem of apparent exceptions which Durkheim will not admit. Here, the criticism of another principle emerges, that the 'same fact cannot have two causes' (Durkheim, 1964b: 83). Finally, having produced a clear definition, and hypothesis, the idea is 'verified' through an analysis of punishment. This verification again demands definition, and relevant characteristics of punishment defined; this definition is used to verify the initial definition of crime. This circle is elaborated at the beginning of the work as an 'hypothesis' – that types of crime and punishment, and therefore law, are symptomatic of different types of social solidarity. The introduction reaches the enunciation of the basic law of the progressive preponderance of the division of labour and restitutive law and the law of the regression of repressive law and mechanical solidarity.

Durkheim then attempts to show the reality of these relationships 'experimentally' (1964b: 133). Here we find a number of comparative series which show: 1. individuals resemble each other more in mechanical societies (133–8); 2. the more that mechanical solidarity dominates the more the law is repressive (138–46); 3. as organic solidarity advances so repressive sanction recedes (156–64); 4. the preponderance of organic solidarity is revealed in the progressive displacement of segmentary structures (183–90); 5. contractual solidarity advances with the division of labour (206–10). There are many dimensions to these series: they are domestic, religious, political, economic, but they all function to demonstrate the tendencies defined in advance by the laws enunciated, as verifications and proofs. Having achieved this impressive array of illustrations, Book Two goes on to examine the causes, and proposes, after having examined three further series (physical/social congregation, concentration, and complexity of communication systems, as well as pure volume itself) that:

> The division of labour varies in direct ratio with the volume and density of societies, and, if it progresses in a continuous manner in the course of social development, it is because societies become regularly denser and generally more voluminous. (1964b: 262)

He then concludes, that 'all these changes are, then, mechanically produced by necessary causes' (273), within already constituted societies (275).

The analysis does not end there. The next section of the argument deals with a whole array of what he calls 'secondary factors', conceived as 'conditions' as distinct from 'causes'. For example, he says, however much the social mass becomes more dense, the tendency to the division of labour will be neutralised by the increasing strength of the collective conscience if that too does not weaken. Another comparative series showing the neutralising effect is given (284–6). But the reality of the transformations in the common conscience is demonstrated with reference to religion (288–90), the weakening of tradition, of regionalism, of gerontocracy, of collective surveillance, and of the domestic milieu and kinship (291–303). The force of heredity also diminishes. The whole of this section is then interpreted relative to the nature of organic solidarity, and is used to draw methodological conclusions: as organic solidarity progresses function becomes increasingly autonomous from organ, secondly it is evident that in analysing social development it is inappropriate to begin from an analysis either of the individual or from an analysis of the social part: 'here, instead, it is the form of all which determines that of the parts' (350).

Finally, Durkheim outlines an analysis of abnormal forms of the division of labour. The analysis does proceed in places through comparisons, but not the ones expected. For example, in the discussion of anomic forms there is a very surprising set of comparisons between the state of the economy and the state of philosophy. The analysis of the forced division of labour is purely abstract.

It is clear then that Durkheim's method completely dominates the organisation of the *Division*; for instance, far from presenting a survey of empirical studies, the work begins with a theoretical discussion of function, of differences and similitudes and so forth, and reaches the conclusion within a few pages that since, in theory, 'law reproduces the principal forms of social solidarity, we have only to classify the different types of law to find therefrom the different types of social solidarity' (1964b: 68). As Durkheim had already presented his idea that there exists only two types of social solidarity reflected in two types of law, the real problem was to establish the relative proportions of each type in any given society; this would then indicate the degree to which the division of labour was developed and this would enable the sociologist to construct an evolutionary series. But this project rests on the reliability of the original dichotomy. It is not entirely true to say that there are no empirical elements given in the attempt to establish it, for Durkheim provides evidence that physiological differences between the sexes arise from specialisation and this difference is the source of conjugal solidarity, and he follows this by providing a formulation of the problem by Comte suggesting that the division of labour produces solidarity. He calls this a hypothesis, which he immediately attempts to verify by saying that, as modern societies with highly developed forms of specialisation exist and possess solidarity, the proposition is really self-evident (1964b: 64), the essential problem is the proportion taken up in any society by this type of solidarity.

Clearly there is a close circle of argument here in which the function of hypothesis, definition, verification, proof and methodological procedures generally seem in danger of merging together. This points to a crucial difficulty in Durkheim's sociology, indicated by many critics (see Chapter Five), concerning his reflection on the precise nature and role of theory in his works. It is not that his sociology is untheoretical, but that the essential theoretical problems appear as *post hoc* rationalisations of single possibilities (for instance that there are only two forms of solidarity) 'verified' by significant examples. If we ask whether the *Division* applies his methodological rules, it is essential to note that his procedures far exceed the specifications of the *Rules* in scope and depth.

TWO LAWS OF PENAL EVOLUTION

By 1901 Durkheim had come to make some quite fundamental rectifications to the analysis undertaken in the *Division,* and these are worked out in the short but, in a methodological sense, classic, essay called 'Two Laws of Penal Evolution' which might be said to follow almost to the letter the method advocated in the *Rules*.

The analysis is called an initial 'gross approximation' to serve as a basis of further investigations. It begins by discussing the first 'law' that intensity of punishments vary with the degree of complexity and organisation of society, but also to the degree that the central power is absolute (Durkheim, 1978: 153). A short theoretical reflection argues that this latter characteristic is not inherent in any given social type (1978: 157); there can be many and various alterations and modifications to the system of government in any society but its basic formation, its species-character, is not thereby transformed: 'The special form of political organisation – governmental absolutism – does not, therefore, arise from the congenital constitution of the society, but from individual, transitory and contingent conditions' (1978: 157). In social evolution the two tendencies, advance of complexity and increasing absolutism, may work in opposite directions, so it may be difficult to follow the quantitative trends precisely.

Having enunciated this law, Durkheim then proposes the evolutionary series to which they conform (1978: 158–64): the sequence includes the following societies: ancient Egypt; Syria; India (Code of Manu); Israel; Athens; Rome (various periods); feudal Europe; absolutist Europe; and modern Europe. The forms of punishment are shown to vary in intensity, negatively with increasing complexity and, positively, with increasing absolutism.

The second law concerns the qualitative variation of the type of punishment which centres more and more on restrictions of freedom. The evolutionary series in this case is a series of legal codes: Code of Manu; Old Testament; Socrates' *The Laws*; Roman law; and mediaeval through to modern legal codes (1978: 164–66) which demonstrate this tendency.

The final sections of the essay attempt 'explications' of these regularities (1978: 166–80). The argument begins with an attempt to show the progressive ways in which the central power is counterbalanced by other social structures which moderate it, while at the same time the means of curtailing liberty in the prison are gradually formed. Turning to the question of the intensity of punishments, Durkheim argues that it is necessary to distinguish between crimes against collectivities (religious crimes) and crimes against individuals (human crimes). The former tend to regress with social evolution, while the latter advance, and 'these two types of criminality differ profoundly because the collective sentiments which they offend are not of the same nature. As a result, repression cannot be the same for both' (1978: 172). The former have the collectivity as their subject (and can be found in each individual) and object:

> In the same way as sensations come to us from the outside world, such sentiments exist within us independent of ourselves and even, to some extent despite ourselves. They become manifest to us in this way as a result of the constraint which they exercise upon us ... crimes which violate these sentiments ... appear exceptionally odious to us. (1978: 173)

In the case of crimes against individuals, the 'distance' between the two sides of the equation has disappeared. The sentiments are not of the same type so 'the very cause which sets in motion the repressive apparatus also tends to impede it', since the punishment is imposed on the individual whose value is raised in the very idea of punishing an offence against the individual. This process of the progressive weakening of punishments with the decline of the awesome powers of the collective being occurs 'mechanically' (1978: 177): and 'though social discipline – of which morality, properly so called is only the highest expression – further extends its field of action, it loses more and more of its authoritarian vigour' (1978: 178). The role of the influence of the power of political organ is explained finally by reference to the balance between the respect for the individual and the respect for the transcendent power incarnated in the state: the more the latter develops the more the repressive mode of sanction prevails over the other: 'which, while less violent and less harsh, still has its own severities and is no way destined to an uninterrupted decline' (1978: 180).

The outline of this article is sufficient to indicate that the method adopted conforms to the 'order of study' specified in the *Rules*: the analysis of covariations conceived on the pattern of a serial comparative analysis, followed by the sociological explanation of such laws. The analysis also raises, acutely, the conception of social species, of the two basic forms of moral sentiments and punishments presented in the *Division*; but it also confirms the conception of such an evolutionary process as occurring 'mechanically', the very term adopted in the *Division*. However, once more the circle of proposition and illustration goes well beyond the formulations of explicit methodology: Durkheim had elided theoretical discussion itself, which functions here as explication of established regularities, instead of acknowledging its formative influence on the construction of both the laws proposed and the genealogies invoked. It appears that the laws have arrived from out of nowhere and are simply confirmed by highly selective illustrations acting as verifications. In explicit methodology, Durkheim had wanted the relations inverted: the construction of impeccable comparisons prior to the induction of regularities.

SUICIDE

Durkheim's interest in the analysis of 'moral statistics' was of long standing by the time *Suicide* was written in 1897. The intention to write this study was announced during 1895 (1978: 181). It is true, however, that a justification for the study of social phenomena through statistics can be found in Durkheim's earliest works and clearly exist in both versions of the *Rules*. There is even one comment in the *Rules* which is a specification of method for the examination of suicide statistics:

> A series can include facts taken from a single, unique society (or from several societies of the same species) or from several distinct species. The first process can, at a pinch, be sufficient when we are dealing with facts of a very general nature about which we have statistical data which are fairly extensive and varied. For instance, by comparing the curve which expresses a suicide trend over a sufficiently extended period of time, with the variations which the same phenomenon exhibits according to provinces, classes, rural or urban environments, sex, age, civil status, etc., we can succeed in establishing real laws without enlarging the scope of our research beyond a single country. Nevertheless, it is always preferable to confirm the results by observations made of other peoples of the same species. (Durkheim, 1982: 155)

Having selected a 'synchronic' approach rather than an evolutionary one, the construction of the series depends on the prospects of being able to vary the statistics for suicides, especially (in the light of the practice in the *Division*) the types of suicide themselves, with the social forms (provinces, classes, etc.) in order to show how the types vary with the social milieux. These would furnish a basis for the penetration of the external indices by sociological analysis to show normal and abnormal phenomena, etc. If the principle of causality is applied in the study of the statistics for France and the modern European nations the sociological analysis could provide a useful indication of their state of health.

But Durkheim prepared some surprises for his readers, especially sociologists trained on the *Rules*, for although, as they would expect, his definition of suicide rests on a specific modification of the commonsense definition (see Giddens, 1972: 32), the project of reaching the causes through analysis of effects is dramatically reversed. The statistics do not permit a classification of the suicide types, an analysis of these has to be achieved indirectly through an analysis of their causes. First must come an analysis of social conditions and situations which must be grouped according to 'their resemblances and differences'. Then, he suggests, 'we shall see that a specific type of suicide will correspond to each of these classes ... instead of being morphological, our classification will from the start be aetiological'. By way of forestalling criticism he added 'nor is this a sign of inferiority, for the nature of a phenomenon is much more profoundly got at by knowing its cause than by knowing its characteristics only, even the most essential ones' (1970: 146–7).

There is an immediate recognition of problems and costs involved in this procedure: the lack of identification of diverse types and special characteristics. But the data on suicides are 'too incomplete and unsure to provide a principle of classification – but once the outlines of a classification are found, the data may be used. They will indicate what direction the deduction should take'. He concludes:

> Thus we shall descend from causes to effects and our aetiological classification will be completed by a morphological one which can verify the former and vice versa.... In all respects this reverse method is the only fitting one for the special problem we have set ourselves. (1970: 147)

There is no real secret then about the method used in *Suicide*: it is *the sociological method used in reverse*, it is described as 'another method' and what is important about it is defined as a reversal of the normal 'order of study' (1970: 146).

This indeed may come as a shock to those who have traditionally regarded *Suicide* as an exemplary application of the *Rules*: it was an application but upside down. The significant idea of this reversal is an opposition not really drawn out in the *Rules*, the opposition between the principle of morphological classification – usually contrasted with physiology – and that of 'aetiological' classification (or classification by causes). In effect the *Suicide* adds a whole chapter to the *Rules* in so far as the concept of such a classification is not identified, nor this new specific order of study analysed. This addition is Chapter One of Book Two of *Suicide*, called 'How to Determine Social Causes and

Social Types'. The method advocated is the 'deduction' of effects from a knowledge of causes. It stands in opposition to the *Division* which is clearly inductivist by comparison.

But the methodological interest of *Suicide* does not rest there, for the chapter called 'Individual Forms of the Different Types of Suicide' (Ch. 6, Book 2), attempts to retrace the ground so as to arrive at a morphological classification of the individual forms by ingeniously combining basic and secondary features. For example, he suggests the basic types are egoistic, altruistic and anomic, and that these are realised in suicides of apathetic, passionate and irritated forms respectively, as their 'fundamental character'. From these might also be identified further more complex forms or 'secondary varieties', e.g. in the case of anomic suicide the instance of violent homicide-suicide. There are further complexities introduced by identification of 'mixed types', e.g. ego-anomic, where the secondary variation is a form specified as a mixture of agitation and apathy. It is certainly a possibility that Durkheim had wanted to start his whole analysis of suicide from these forms, the morphology itself, and then to have worked towards an analysis of causes. He may have also tried to find the causes from an analysis of the means by which suicides had been accomplished (Table xxx, 1970: 291), but was to discover no reliable continuity between the means and the character of the suicide. The whole construction of the individual form in this chapter reveals in an interesting way precisely what Durkheim meant by the complexity of such forms and the difficulty of taking them as a starting point. It also illuminates the 'causal principle' outlined in the *Rules,* for here it is clear that if each effect has its own specific cause, there is also the fact that a phenomenon may be the complex outcome of the combination of more than one cause, i.e., as a complex effect.

EDUCATIONAL THOUGHT

Durkheim's lectures on educational practice in France are also clearly in line with the general framework of evolutionary sociology, since the whole set of educational courses contain attempts to adumbrate an evolutionary series from which to deduce the pattern of normal development, and hence to aid the formation of educational policy. But these lectures, *Educational Thought,* dispense almost entirely with the formal apparatus of propositions, verifications, and proofs. The lectures were not presented as a course in sociology but a course in

the history of higher education in France. Nevertheless, this massive
course clearly deals with the relation between educational ideals and
the institutional framework in various epochs (which form as such an
evolutionary sequence). The project aimed at the identification of
major deficiencies in the structure of the curriculum, which he took to
imply the existence of pathological phenomena, the most interesting
being Durkheim's attempt to analyse the defects in the system brought
about by the wholesale destruction of the mediaeval corpus by the
reforms of the Renaissance, and the rise in the latter epoch of widespread physical violence in the schools and colleges. In his early lectures
on moral education (1898) Durkheim suggested that it was with the
emergence of the school as a special institution, the organised meeting
of adults and children outside of the family that the inevitable infliction
of violence on children in a systematic way began. As schools became
more independent in ancient Rome the use of the *ferula* and the
flagellum increased; in the Middle Ages discipline became even more
intense, especially with the rise of the monastic schools reaching a
peak in the thirteenth century when the 'lash, particularly, played such
a part that it became a sort of idol'; in the Renaissance there was
continuous protest from writers like Rabelais, Erasmus and
Montaigne, but the lash remained in use up until the eighteenth
century.

By the time Durkheim had researched his 1904 lectures, *Educational
Thought,* he had reorganised this 'evolution'. The idea that the schools
and colleges of the Middle Ages were characterised by harsh and
inhuman violence was now judged a legend constructed in the Renaissance. Only children below the age of twelve in the grammar classes
were the object of physical discipline. Other than this, he said, not
until 'the end of the fifteenth century do we find any trace of corporal
punishment'. Even after 1450, when certain exceptional measures of a
repressive type were established, the basic pattern was one of leniency.
The fundamental reason for this was that the educational communities
remained essentially democratic in organisation, and democratic
organisations imply that 'he who is today judged may tomorrow
become the judge' (Durkheim, 1977: 155–7). The analysis seizes hold
of the fact that the turn towards a more oppressive system began
at the turn of the sixteenth century just at the moment when the
schools and colleges became centralised and cut off from the outside
community. Students at this time suffered a considerable loss of status
and restriction of liberty. The growth of despotism and closure to

public surveillance in the context of a new demarcation of statuses inside the colleges meant that the conditions were ripe for the emergence of the whip 'as a regular part of college life'.

The way that this story unfolds is related to important sociological observations. For example, the emergence of the Renaissance itself is discussed. In opposition to the idea that it was caused by the rediscovery of the culture of antiquity, he suggested it was related to the profound changes of European society itself. As we have already seen with the analysis of the breakdown of the medieval synthesis, the period of the renaissance seems to reveal many symptoms of social crisis. These are again developed in these lectures where the basic signs of anomie (pathological structures of desire for unattainable ends), class crystallisation, destruction of basic forms of solidarity, growth of violent practices, emergence of absolutism, etc., are all detailed. It is important to note, however, that this work does not construct a comparative sociological series by reference to theoretical levels of complexity and organisation: it is a continuous historical series, and it is significant that Durkheim himself called it a 'history' (Halbwachs, in Durkheim, 1977: xi, 13, 16; cf., Durkheim 1973: 184–7).

ELEMENTARY FORMS

The final major work which can be considered here is *The Elementary Forms of the Religious Life* of 1912. This work is a long and detailed analysis of Australian totemism, a subject that had long interested Durkheim (for example, see the mention in the *Division* (1964b: 432)). In the *Forms* Durkheim was to attack the problem both as an object of the sociology of religion and the sociology of knowledge (1961: 13–33).

As expected, perhaps, Durkheim proceeds by discussing the 'external' characteristics and 'signs' by which religious phenomena can be recognised, grouped together and made the object of a critical sociological experiment. As in other studies, the relation of 'external' and 'internal' phenomena is posed as a necessary assumption of such investigations:

> Since all religions can be compared to each other, and since all are species of the same class, there are necessarily many elements which are common to all. We do not mean to speak simply of the outward and visible characteristics which they all have equally, and which make it possible to give them a provisional definition at the outset of our researches; the discovery of these

apparent signs is relatively easy, for the observation which it demands does not go beyond the surface of things.

This confirms the view that such initial work is highly provisional. 'But these external resemblances suppose others which are profound ... How is it possible to pick them out?' (1961: 17). Durkheim's answer is to suggest that it is necessary to select the case where religious phenomena are found in their most 'elementary' and indeed 'simplest' form: then the elements are easier to 'disengage' and relationships are visibly more 'apparent' (1961: 19). The more complex societies are cases where the original sources of religion are somewhat remote:

> The psychological gap between the cause and the effect, between the apparent cause and the effective cause, has become more considerable ... The remainder of this book will be an illustration and a verification of this remark on method. It will be seen how, in primitive religions, the religious fact still visibly carries the mark of its origins. (1961: 20)

Again, Durkheim recommends the comparative method, but on condition that it is used judiciously: he warns against 'tumultuous and summary comparisons'. Comparisons are, he suggests, in a comment directly in opposition to the formulation of the *Rules* (1982: 156), only appropriate within specific social types: exterior resemblances must be controlled by making sure that they have the same sense and significance relative to each social type (Durkheim, 1961: 114). The aim here is to reach a situation where a limited number of relevant facts can be selected for even 'one single fact may make a law appear'. In this perspective the choice of Australian totemism is eminently justified for the facts are 'homogeneous', and the most elementary (1961: 113–15). And, at the end of the work, he returned to this theme to claim that the book had indeed been such an experiment (1961: 462–3).

Durkheim had in fact attempted to reach an adequate definition of religion many years before. In an article of 1899 he had suggested that 'phenomena held to be religious consist in obligatory beliefs connected with clearly defined practices which are related to given objects of those beliefs' (in Durkheim 1975b, 93). By 1912 Durkheim had come to think this inadequate: it 'was too formal, and neglected the contents of the religious representations too much ... moreover, if their imperative character is really a distinctive trait of religious beliefs, it allows of an infinite number of degrees. There are even cases where it is not easily perceptible' (Durkheim, 1961: 63). Durkheim thus recommended the following as more adequate:

> A religion is a unified system of beliefs and practices relative to sacred things, that is to say, things set apart and forbidden – beliefs and practices which unite into one single moral community called a church, all those who adhere to them. (1961: 62)

Here the element of 'obligation' has been eliminated, and the ideas of the systematic nature of the connection of beliefs and practices, and the specification of religious objects as sacred, have been added together with the idea that these produce a single community morally united. Thus the two poles of Durkheim's sociology are combined again. But what gives this definition undeniable potency is the introduction of the idea of the sacred, a category which fuses two aspects of belief structures, that is as a moral reality and a category of social knowledge. In considering collective representations Durkheim thus seems to replace 'moral obligation' with what he calls 'logical necessity' (1961), but in fact he clearly insists that this is not a replacement but an addition to his previous analysis. (He notes this by signalling the fact that society itself recognises the difference between abnormally low intelligence and delinquency, i.e., between facts of consciousness and of conscience.) It would certainly be tempting to suggest that the introduction of the socially constitutive nature of such categories indicates a dramatic transformation of a declaration of the *Rules,* which said that the sociologist must shake off 'once and for all, the yoke of those empirical categories that long habit often makes tyrannical' (Durkheim, 1982: 73). Durkheim now says 'the necessity with which the categories are imposed upon us is not the effect of simple habits whose yoke we could easily throw off with a little effort ... it is a special sort of moral necessity which is to the intellectual life what moral obligation is to the will' (Durkheim, 1961: 30). The temptation should be resisted, especially in light of the observation in the *Rules* that prenotions do have a specific resistance to human will in their own right (Durkheim, 1982: 63). The development from the period of the early 1890s is more to be found in the rejection of the view presented in *Division* that the culture of primitive societies is based on sensation not on concepts (Durkheim, 1964b: 290).

What Durkheim appears to do in 1912 is to connect the idea of working from the exterior to the interior of social facts with the idea of working from the exterior to the interiority of collective representation:

PART ONE

'Outside of us there is public opinion which judges us; but more than that, since society is also represented inside of us, it sets itself against these revolutionary fancies, even inside of ourselves.' The way that society is represented on the inside is through the action of social 'fundamental categories': time, space, logical class, force, personality, efficacy, even contradiction (Durkheim, 1961: 21–5). If this really is the case, these categories 'should depend upon the way in which (the group) is founded and organised, upon its morphology, upon its religious, moral and economic institutions, etc.' Durkheim seeks not only to suggest that the sacred is a fundamental social category, but that the other fundamental categories are 'of religious origin' (1961: 33). The apparently universal and absolute division between sacred and profane is then subjected to sociological analysis itself. It is necessary to point out here that some commentators have suggested that Durkheim's later position is close to 'maintaining that symbolic thought is a condition of and explains society' (Lukes, 1973: 235). It must be emphasised that his position, as is presented in *Forms,* is that collective representations are a constituent structure of all human society, but that religious representations are a constituent feature of the first societies, and that where these persist so do the social structures which give rise to them. The basic comparative series here, hardly noticed in the flow of Durkheim's discourse, is the juxtaposition of the opposition of sacred/profane with the opposition of social concentration/social dispersal. And so the work has discovered, he says:

some of the elements out of which the most fundamental religious notions are made up.... If among certain peoples the ideas of sacredness, the soul and God are to be explained sociologically, it should be presumed scientifically that, in principle, the same explanation is valid for all the peoples among whom these same ideas are found with the same essential characteristics. (1961: 462–3)

Durkheim concludes that 'however simple the system' found in Australia, it is possible to find within it 'all the great ideas and the principal ritual attitudes' which are found at the base of all, 'even the most advanced' religions. Religions are not created by 'mere ideas', but out of the cult and its combined material and mental operations (Durkheim, 1961: 464). But religious representations have two sides, they are both categorical and construct ideals, thus 'far from ignoring the real society, (are) in its image' (1961: 468), while such a 'collective consciousness is something more than a mere epiphenomenon of its

56

morphological basis ... this synthesis has the effect of disengaging a whole world of sentiments, ideas and images which, once born, obey laws all their own' (1961: 471); a thesis to be found incidentally in the second preface in the *Rules* (Durkheim, 1982: 41).

The main difficulty here was already identified by Durkheim in a paper of 1898 where he specifically noted the problem of thinking 'social facts as phenomena produced *in* but also *by* the society'. The problem exists, he suggested, because there are social facts which are produced 'not by the society but by already formed social products'. Durkheim posited a hierarchy of social facts themselves: there are some fundamental and primary ones which are produced organically as part of its immediate structure and functioning, others are of the 'second degree' and governed by their relatively autonomous laws of collective ideation (Durkheim, 1953: 32). (That Durkheim preserves here the order of primary and secondary phenomena without reducing the second to the first is significantly different from the idea that he argues that 'symbolic thought ... explains society' (Lukes, 1973).)

It is important, however, to remember that there are two basic conjoint objects of study in *Forms*: sociology of religion and sociology of knowledge. If Durkheim applies his rules to the study of the first – examining the beliefs and rituals together as a structure of practices created by the rhythms and dynamics of the social body, its morphology and its cult – he adds that this sociology of religion can be interpreted by a sociology of knowledge. At the close of the work, the concluding sections might well be expected to contain propositions concerning the concomitant variation of totemism and clan-based society, the possible variations in other religious forms with more complex social structures, and indeed such a comparative series is sketched. But the sociology of knowledge intervenes in a curious way. Durkheim appears to want to forego a full analysis and attempt to move from such external issues to consider more directly the internal structures revealed. These are approached in a preliminary 'interpretation' of the relation of religion and knowledge, but not in relation to what appear as 'obligatory' practices, i.e., as a result of covariation of external characteristics. It is the analysis of the structure of the cult which is the object of interpretation. The analytic process has this form: through the application of the rules of method to the study of the external features of the elementary cult, an analysis has been produced which can then figure as a means by which the internal structures (those not perceived as externally constraining) can be known. Thus a miraculous sort of complicity has been revealed between, on the one hand, the externality of moral obligations and the internality of social categories, and, on the other, the externality of surface representation of things prior to scientific analysis and the knowledge of the internal connections of things achieved by science. But more than this: from this experiment a legitimate induction can be made concerning the more advanced societies. Durkheim has carefully prepared this move: science itself reflects in its structure the nature of the more advanced societies and it begins to replace religious representations in social evolution, but as it does so it maintains the unity of category and ideal. It is no surprise to learn here that scientific reason does not replace morality, but brings its own.

At the end of this work Durkheim appeals, as he did in the Introduction to the *Division* and the first chapter of the *Rules,* to the reader in the first person. He reiterates the idea that even space and time are twofold: individual and social. This latter order is 'imposed on all minds and all events' (Durkheim, 1961: 490). Society alone engenders these categories as representations which transcend, infinitely, the experiences of the individual: the 'world is inside society' (1961: 490). The drama which unfolds in the final pages of this work is the scene of the breakdown of the old categories in the face of the changing nature of society: 'a new sort of life is developing' so that 'things can no longer be contained in the social moulds according to which they were primitively classified' (1961: 493).

5

Durkheim's Sociology

It would be instructive to investigate the methodological positions adopted by Durkheim's close associates: for example, the essays by Mauss, Fauconnet, Hubert, Hertz and others, written soon after, and under the direct influence, of the *Rules*. These essays possess a common style of working, and an emerging common set of themes, even a basic common theory, which depart somewhat, as would be expected, from Durkheim's own. In general they are less ambitious in scope, remaining within what might now be conceived as the orbit of anthropology. A number of large scale evolutionary studies were no doubt undertaken during this period which remained uncompleted and unpublished, others were published only after Durkheim's death. What was completed seemed to be synthesised selectively by Durkheim into the argument of the *Elementary Forms* which I have discussed elsewhere (Gane, 1983a, 1983b). Here I will select a number of key elements of Durkheim's own approach to try to identify its most important characteristic perspectives.

Sociology, for Durkheim, should strive for complete independence from all purely partisan interests; this could best be achieved by situating it in the context of the institutions of higher education and integrating it as far as possible among the sciences. This new science did not appear out of thin air but had a true lineage which he traced in his more official methodological pronouncements as the genealogy leading from Aristotle, through Montesquieu, to Comte and Spencer. In some formulations it appears as if the decisive figure of modern times as far as methodology was concerned was Montesquieu – 'his successors in instituting *sociology,* did little more than give a name to the field of study he inaugurated' (Durkheim, 1965: 57). However, it was Saint-Simon who gave sociology its principal content: 'he not only laid out its design but attempted to realise it in part' (1962: 143). But another, crucial formulation suggests 'it is from Condorcet and the encyclopaedists that Saint-Simon, Comte and all the positive philosophy of the nineteenth century derive' (Durkheim, 1977: 293). Durkheim claimed that Marxism had no influence at all on the formation of his sociology.

Methodologically, there were two principal influences on sociology: the idea of productive or 'efficient' causation itself (and the idea that each effect must be thought to have a single cause) derived from the physical sciences, and the theme of reproductive or 'functional' causation (derived from the biological or life sciences). The principles of evolutionary biology were to form the scaffolding of the new social science and were not to intervene as substantive ideas in social analysis. The major difference between Marx and Durkheim here was that whereas Marx saw the social scientist as playing the role of 'midwife' to the new order in the chain of social evolution, Durkheim rejected the idea that the 'next stage' was implied in the previous one and was even predictable (Durkheim, 1982: 140). This gave Durkheim's sociology its apparently conservative complexion: the role of the social scientist was to know how what exists can be brought to a higher state of well-being. Against the view that knowledge should simply attempt to approach the natural perfection in which everything exists, and against the view (actually closely associated with the former) that considerations of fact and value should be kept completely separate, Durkheim postulated what he considered a far more complex idea, common in the life sciences – the idea of health and pathology: the objective of the sociologist was to determine as far as possible the healthy norm, the practice of the sociologist was not to act as midwife (it can be seen that his position implies a basic critique of this metaphor, since the midwife is engaged in a process not of the production of a new species, but in the reproduction of the old) but as general physician to society, to restore it to its normal state in times of illness. Durkheim expressed this theoretically in the curious phrase as by 'comparing the normal type with itself ... we shall be able to find if it is not entirely in agreement with itself' (1984: 34).

This complex of procedures was, then, conceived as an application of scientific rationalism, of positive science, that had therapeutic aims in view. In part these aims were linked with the internal division in the science – of the study of normal and pathological phenomena, which can be seen as requiring the construction of a table of normal social types for this was in fact the key to sociology being able to produce any effective practical conclusions. Here Durkheim followed a position that owes something to Saint-Simon, who reversed the dominant modern view (derived from the Renaissance) that the medieval period was a superstitious, violent and simple age, suggesting instead that it was precisely the flowering of medieval culture which witnessed the creation of modern organic social structures, especially around the emergence of secondary corporate formations (e.g. the Universities, etc.). Durkheim thus argued that the normal forms of modern European societies should be as balanced as the equivalent medieval ones: his emergent political diagnosis was that some form of development of institutions similar to the guilds was essential. His analysis of suicide rates ended with an attempt to show that they were abnormally high because the fundamental structures of occupational solidarity were insufficient in modern societies; his analysis of educational institutions ended with the call to restore elements of dialectic to the curriculum partly because they had played a vital role in the medieval university.

Durkheim's view of what modern society should be like has been called 'institutional socialism' (see Gane, 1984), and in a sense all of his major projects were aimed at showing in one way or another what it was and why it was necessary to work towards it. But not through either a simple restoration of the medieval guild system (Durkheim, 1962: 168) or revolutionary erasure of all existing institutions. It involved, he argued, a complex transformation, of restoration, conservation and removal, if the oscillation of tyranny and revolutionary anarchism was to be halted. Hence he objected to the utopian tradition stemming from Saint-Simon which wanted to return to a simpler form of stateless society, for example. On the other hand he was not a straightforward reformist since his theory of collective effervescences held that it was only through such vast but creative social upheavals that social morality was reborn. Durkheim, the rationalist, in the end followed Saint-Simon and Comte in the sense that he saw a new socialist morality as requiring all the formal elements of a cult.

There seems to be a latent controversy over interpretation of Durkheim's view of the nature of this cult. Steven Lukes, for example, in drawing up an 'ideal type' version of Durkheim's conception of organic solidarity described the content of the *conscience collective* as 'abstract and general' (Lukes, 1973: 158). It seems to me more likely that the content was envisioned to be (and here, as did Marx and Engels, he followed Saint-Simon) scientific sociology itself, just as 'scientific socialism' was to be the content of Marxist envisioned societies. Whereas Marx and Engels saw the union of theory and class politics as the motor for the achievement of socialism, Durkheim saw class formation as a part of the very pathological breakdown he wanted to overcome, and any subordination of theory to class politics would jeopardise its function. It was to the University, to a certain extent 'above class conflicts' (1976: 387), that Durkheim looked, and this was certainly consistent with his view that it was in developing such corporate institutions real social progress was to be made.

So Durkheim's evolutionism did not become the springboard of an attempt to identify a trend or even the next stage of a progressive chain. It was the framework, however, not only of a search for the normal and pathological but for the operation of further borrowed concepts: of physiology and morphology, structure and function, which were set to work on the basis of an application of the principal emergent evolutionary properties in nature more generally. Just as biological phenomena were based on combinations of inorganic material, and psychological were based on the biological, so social phenomena represented a distinct domain of irreducible facts to which scientific methods of understanding could be applied in principle. Standing in the way of such an effort were a number of obstacles primary among which were the individualist humanist assumptions of the everyday world. Tracing a route very similar to that of Marx, Durkheim sought to provide a critique of the epistemological pretensions of humanism. But, like Marx in fact, his theory did not eliminate 'the individual', it aimed, in the first instance, to overturn normal expectations:

> We do not support the thesis that morality among the living has no aspect that is individual, but the social aspect is the principal part, and it is with the social side that we must come to grips first if we would understand what is behind the other. It is not a question of denying one of the two points of view at the expense of the other, but of reversing the order of preponderance between them that is accepted through habit. (Durkheim, 1980: 144)

As is clear from the conspectus of the *Rules*, a major reform of perspective is required if the project is to be successful, but its object is a revolution in human knowledge comparable to the process in psychology:

In the end, the reform that must be introduced into sociology is identical in every respect to that which has transformed psychology over the last thirty years ... states of consciousness must be studied externally and not from the perspective of the individual consciousness which experiences it. This is the great revolution that has been accomplished in this field. (Durkheim, 1982: 71)

PART TWO

Deus traditit munum hominum disputationi

(often cited by Durkheim, e.g. 1962:233; 1961:477; 1977:152, etc.)

6

Introduction: the *Rules* and the Sociologists

A number of comments can be made about the kind of debate that has ensued over the *Rules* since 1894. Evidently a large number of different kinds of arguments have taken place. One thing, however, stands out above everything else: that apart from those who were in direct contact with Durkheim and his team around the *Année,* there has been only one basic judgment about its merit: the book is, as a statement of principles, highly defective. It has been thought illusory, even a complete delusion, as well as politically dangerous. It is widely believed that Durkheim himself treated the whole exercise more as a conceit, or a territorial claim, while his actual method was something completely at odds with his 'official' method. Many of the commentaries have sought to examine the work in the context of Durkheim's own development. The significance of the *Rules* thus varies from the status of an early but marginal synthesis, after which the real break occurred in 1898 (Parsons, Lukes), or as a precursor of a break which occurred in 1895 (Lacroix), or indeed the *Rules* makes the break with the very first chapter of the work itself in 1894 (Alexander). Others have taken strong exception to this kind of analysis and we should note Giddens's dissention: 'the conventional interpretation ... is that Durkheim moved from the relatively 'materialistic' position which he is presumed to have held in the *Division* towards a standpoint much closer to 'idealism' ... this is misleading if not wholly fallacious' (Giddens, 1971: 105).

Many of the readings have sought to contest the definition given by Durkheim of the social fact: a 'mediaeval realism' (Tarde), 'relational realism' (Alpert), 'radical sociologistic positivism' (Parsons), etc. The question of Durkheim's attempt to identify a non-substantive objectivity with his conception of society as an emergent property seems not to have lost its fascination for sociologists. Nor has Durkheim's flirtation with the language of empiricism, functionalism, and structuralism. On the other hand, some have thought his position a subjectivism or even mysticism. But one of the favourite sports of Durkheim critics has been the attempt to spot the logical contradictions in the first chapters of the *Rules*. Giddens, for example, thinks that there is an apparent contradiction between the idea stated at the beginning of the *Rules* that everyone 'drinks, sleeps, eats' but this does not make them social facts (Durkheim, 1982: 50) with the illustration of individuals having been taught to 'eat, drink and sleep' at regular intervals as social facts (Durkheim, 1982: 54). Marshall Sahlins argues that to say education imposes ways of thinking and acting is inconsistent with Durkheim's suggestion that our ideas are representations of things derived from sense experience (Sahlins, 1976: 110). But apparent contradictions would not have worried Durkheim says Robert Nisbet, for example, he 'was relentlessly rationalist and scientific in methodology', yet his thought has an 'umbilical relationship' with early nineteenth century conservatism (Nisbet 1965: 28).

7

The Debate Over the *Rules* in Recent British Sociology

As one might expect, there are some highly diligent attempts to introduce and to precis the *Rules* so as to make its ideas available to students and to a wide popular audience. The best of these in recent British sociology (for example, Ronald Fletcher (1971, Vol. 2, section 2A) or Anthony Giddens (1971: Ch. 6; 1972: 29–38; 1978: Ch. 2) are accurate and well balanced. But even in these authors, major problems arise when simple presentation moves on to assessment and criticism. When Durkheim says he wants to introduce a specifically scientific approach into the study of social facts, Fletcher expostulates that this is an utterly fatuous attempt to clamber 'ever more frantically up a gum tree'. For Durkheim, says Fletcher, the only truth seems to be scientific truth, a 'dogmatic scientism which clothed inaccuracies and logical errors' (Fletcher, 1971; Vol. 2, 288, 299). In the end Durkheim's inconsistencies in dealing with such problems as teleology intruded inescapably into his 'science', for how could he advocate an antivoluntaristic sociology if not voluntaristically?

Although the account of Durkheim given by Anthony Giddens in the early 1970s is a far more subtle one, his later conclusion as to the status of the *Rules* specifically is that it is riddled with internal inconsistencies and contradictions and is seemingly based on a completely 'uncritical' acceptance of a 'crudely empiricist stance' (Giddens, 1977: 292). One of the most recent social theory textbooks cites Durkheim's definition of the social fact and remarks, in the tone of most introductory texts, 'now this will not do!' (Lee and Newby, 1983: 214).

Certainly one of the most influential presentations of Durkheim in

Britain in the early 1960s was the work of John Rex. For him there was no doubt about the predominantly empiricist orientation of this work by Durkheim. It was manifest in its lack of discussion of the importance of the need for a 'clear and specifically sociological frame of reference guiding the formulation of hypotheses' (Durkheim, 1970: 27). When Durkheim begins to investigate any particular terrain of social facts, it is suggested, he is forced to accept the reality of these facts as given by the individual human participants themselves. This is inevitable and indeed 'there would be no harm in this if he were to recognise what he is doing' (1970: 45). But Durkheim appears to believe that what he is working on is a raw material of a purely natural kind. This reality, identified by Durkheim as a 'group mind' means that he is guilty of illegitimately hypostatising the product of human inter-action into a thing. The unfortunate consequence of such reification is that the real object of sociological inquiry, the social relationship itself, is obscured from view. If Durkheim had started from the real social relation, the resulting concept of society would not have taken on any mystical overtones (1970: 50).

In the 1970s this kind of criticism broadened. An example of it can be found in the writings of Ted Benton, who argued:

... the identification of the 'object of knowledge' or 'subject matter' of a science can only occur in the course of the production of knowledge of it ... The limits and scope of its applicability of concepts cannot be given in advance of the system of concepts itself, they are rather an aspect of the specification of the concepts. In short, Durkheim's whole attempt to establish a 'space' for the autonomous discipline of sociology is vitiated by its defective, empiricist conception of the relation between a science and its subject matter. This is, of course, not to argue that Durkheim errs in deriving the definition of the social from 'pure observation'. Rather, he errs in presenting his argument in this form, and submerging the *real* source of his conception of social facts, which is a general philosophy of nature ... Underlying these latter, 'given' concepts are the everyday, pre-scientific notions of 'social order' and 'consensus' which are constitutive of the political project which Durkheim's work theorises. (Benton, 1977: 89)

Here, under the influence of modern epistemological theory (specifically Althusserian), the meaning of the term empiricist has changed slightly to refer now to the way in which a subject draws knowledge from an object. The argument is fundamentally the same, however, i.e., that Durkheim does not adequately present the theoretical conditions for the elaboration of scientific knowledge.

A more recent consideration suggests that Durkheim's principal strategy is a rationalist one but that in the *Rules* he appears to present a methodology which is at variance with this and in this text adopts a position which is naively empiricist (Johnson, et al., 1984: Ch. 5). Certainly Durkheim himself wanted to adopt the label 'rationalist' for his general orientation, but Johnson et al. give the term an unusually wide meaning – to include any view which maintains that the social is ideal rather than material, where the mode of validation is logical rather than empirical, and which rejects the distinction between fact and value, adhering in its place to an ethical absolutism. The position in the *Rules* is said to be 'rather simple' – a recommendation that the sociologist proceed from 'facts' to 'ideas', from the external to the internal via the use of the comparative method. But, it is suggested, this puts empiricist inductivism and rationalism into contradiction. The analysis concludes that 'There is little doubt that in his sociological analysis elsewhere Durkheim does not use the methods he advocates in the *Rules* ... and the *Rules* does not even accord with the whole drift of what he took to be the nature of sociology.' The whole effort of the exposition of the *Rules* is misplaced and forms an aberrant moment in what is otherwise a consistent rationalist enterprise.

Many of the same arguments criticising Durkheim can be found in the work of Paul Hirst but under different names. Hirst stigmatises the work as 'realist', even 'ultra-realist', while being based on a thorough-going rejection of rationalism (Hirst, 1975: 100, 113). He says: 'Durkheim had no conception of the rationalism entailed in the materialism of science'. If Durkheim does attempt, he argues, to take up and work on social facts which are in the field of the immediately available objects in the social world, all that really happens is that in the conceptual manipulations that make them appear for sociology, i.e., in the process by which they are selected and elaborated, an already given idea of what they are as inherently moral entities is illegitimately inserted. Hirst, attempting to follow Bachelard, defines realism as a doctrine which specifies its object as a range of things which appear to have 'reality' for the observer. As this is certainly a definition at variance with the dominant Anglo-Saxon philosophical usage, and Durkheim's himself of course, some caution must be applied here. Hirst's argument is that Durkheim's realism is the platform from which a terrain of social phenomena comes into view in a process apparently uncontaminated by theoretical or ideological preconceptions. This, according to Hirst, is the hidden 'trick' Durkheim is able to use in order to pose as a scientific sociologist (Hirst, 1975: 107). When, subsequently, the process of theoretical analysis is added to this trick, Durkheim's 'own realist theory of knowledge is contradicted' (1975: 107). Hirst's conclusions are:

Durkheim's attempt to create a scientific sociology could not but be a failure. Durkheim's sociology is as impossible as the epistemology on which is founded, and, far from being a science, it is a mechanism for the rationalisation of phenomena given to it by political and social ideologies. (Hirst, 1975: 167)

At base, says Hirst, Durkheim's sociological project is nothing other than a simplistic sociologism/psychologism, or better: individualism/holism theoretical 'couple' held in place by the obscure energy of a mystic vitalism.

Another influential reading of the *Rules* in the early 1970s suggested that it was really a manifesto of sociological positivism. This idea was developed by David Walsh, who argued that however sophisticated Durkheim's conception of social facts might be 'what is missing in Durkheim's account is some actual analysis of the processes by which the structure of social interaction produces an emergent social reality' (in Filmer, et al., 1972: 37). The process by which the gestures and meanings which originate in the individual members of a society are shared and take on the character of socially structured relations is left entirely to one side, he suggests. This reflects an assumption about the already given level of meaningful action in society which seems not to be the object of special study and explanation. It forms, indeed, an unexamined set of materials which in fact is taken, uncritically, for granted, although it is the starting point of sociological exploration. But there is a certain vascillation on Durkheim's part, in that he does postulate that the inner structures of society are a form of social consciousness. The problem arises, then, because this central object is approached as if it were a 'disembodied' thing (1972: 38). Positivism, which is regarded here as a mode of thought which specifically reduces human objects to the status of natural ones, misses the real object of social analysis, which must be to establish exactly how this apparently given level of meaning itself comes into existence (1972: 55). One of the most influential sociology textbooks of recent years adopted his label to classify Durkheim's work (Haralambos, 1980: 495).

The most recent work to appear which considers this label ends by suggesting that Durkheim is indeed, despite all protestations, a 'maximalist positivist' (Bryant, 1985: 56). Bryant tries to adumbrate a

fairly wide definition of positivism (combining definitions of Kolakowski and Giddens (Bryant, 1985: 1–10), but, even so, he has considerable
difficulty in explaining how the *Rules* is embraced by it. He has to
argue at one point that because Durkheim is regarded as a positivist
'perhaps even the most celebrated, or notorious, of all positivists',
there must be something in the charge even if it is not 'sensitive enough
to capture the highly distinctive character of Durkheim's positivism'.
This specific character, according to Bryant, can be identified in Durkheim's general anti-empiricist position ('despite some infelicities of
drafting in the *Rules*'), the insistence on society as a reality in its own
right, a dual epistemology which accepts a pragmatic view: first identify
what is valid, then add a correspondence theory of truth; he also
had little interest in empirical research techniques, but showed much
interest in a science of morals and worked for a positivist polity. All
these, according to Bryant, are the classic elements of French positivism. On the *Rules* specifically, Bryant finds it replete with inconsistencies and contradictions, and indeed repeats many of the
observations already listed above. His discussion concludes:

> Durkheim instructs us in the *Rules* to disregard preconceptions and to attend
> directly to things. He then finds himelf having to concede that we cannot
> attend directly to things, that to get scientific investigation started we have to
> have recourse to preconceptions. Once investigation in a particular field is
> underway, however, he expects scientific concepts to displace pre-scientific
> ones; and if he now alludes to a trichotomy of preconceptions (ordinary
> collective representations), scientific concepts (superior collective rep-
> resentations of a special type) and reality itself, he still supposes that scientific
> concepts are derived from things themselves, even though he does not offer
> any theory of scientific concept formation which would indicate how this feat
> is achieved and even though his own illustrations in the *Rules*, and his practice
> elsewhere, would not have appeared to achieve it. (Bryant, 1985: 40)

In the mid-1970s two influential works which considered Durkheim's positivism both sought to offer certain qualifications. Barry
Smart for example noted that:

> Durkheim's methodological proposal that social facts be treated as things
> seems to have been transformed within sociology and taken to infer that
> social facts are things. . . . We should be careful to avoid misrepresenting or
> misinterpreting. . . . (Smart, 1976: 78)

While Keat and Urry suggested that:

For Durkheim, and for the other positivists, there is the strongest desire to reject the suggestion that mysterious metaphysical or theological forces are responsible for producing the contours of the empirically observable world.... Yet, when positivists seek to put into operation their methodology they often find themselves employing realist arguments or positing realist-like entities.... [But] there are various reasons why we do not think his approach is realist. First, Durkheim aims to discover through Millian causes the essence of the phenomena.... Second, the realist does not identify such essences, or underlying structures, by Durkheim's curious method of definition; namely classing together all phenomena that happen to share certain common external characteristics. Third, while Durkheim links together a single cause and single effect, the realist argues that any such effect results from the complex interrelations between mechanisms, structures and background conditions. (Keat and Urry, 1984)

Thus Durkheim is 'part-positivist and part-essentialist': 'our view is basically that Durkheim's position is ambiguous' (Keat and Urry, 2nd ed., 1982: 85–6).

Finally, as a general, if not entirely representative verdict on this work by Durkheim, the 'Introduction' by Steven Lukes to the new translation of 1982, reveals something of the kind of status it now seems to enjoy. Unlike the introduction to the 1938 translation, which saw the work as pro-fascist (Durkheim, 1964a: xxviii), Lukes recognises Durkheim's liberal socialist orientations. Apart from this, the essay is one of pure denunciation. Durkheim's edifice rests on 'unexamined and shaky foundations' because it lacks a hermeneutic underpinning. The method is found 'contradictory', 'not feasible', 'obsessed', 'limiting', 'distorting', 'insensitive', 'narrow', 'makes little sense', 'distinctly crude', 'unclear', 'highly implausible', 'illusory', 'flawed', 'misconceived', 'dogmatic' and – 'sterile'. Lukes adds 'Durkheimian dogma has proved a powerfully productive and progressive research programme' – in spite of the *Rules*.

8

The Storm Over the *Rules* in France During Durkheim's Lifetime

'When this book first appeared, it aroused some fairly lively controversy' (Durkheim, 1982: 34). On the one hand, of course, there was support for the project from Durkheim's friends and collaborators in the informal circles forming around the *Année Sociologique* from the mid 1890s, though even here there were some who had some deep misgivings about Durkheim's definition of a social fact (see, for example, letters between Durkheim and Bouglé in Besnard, P., 1983: 40–2). There were also supporters of the essay and Durkheim's larger programme, such as Georges Sorel, who were keen to show that there were close parallels between this genre of sociology and Marxism. Durkheim was concerned to keep these supporters at arms length. On the other hand there was a torrent of criticism, some of it highly venomous, culminating in the charge made by Jean Izoulet – Professor of Social Philosophy at the Collège de France – that the teaching of Durkheim's doctrine was 'the gravest national peril that our country has known for some time' (cited in Clark, 1973: 194).

Much of this criticism was inspired by views based on conceptions which appealed, explicitly, to the fundamental importance of individual experience, historical experience, and philosophical nominalism, but there was also criticism from Catholic moralists and socialist and anarchist activists. Fortunately there exists not only a large number of critical essays, many of which have been translated, but also actual debates between the leading representatives of these tendencies which were transcribed and published at the time.

In this chapter I will focus on a number of such confrontations: the encounters particularly with Gabriel Tarde, Simon Deploige, Charles Seignobos, Alfred Fouillée and Georges Sorel.

GABRIEL TARDE

'There are few sociological truths as useful to examine as Mr Durkheim's errors,' Tarde announced in 1894 (1969: 120). Born in 1843, Tarde reached the high point of his career as sociology became highly fashionable in the 1890s and as Durkheim's work, especially the *Rules*, had begun to be widely read by a new popular audience. They were in direct and open competition and it was Tarde, with a background in criminology, sociology and philosophy, who was appointed to the chair of philosophy (over Bergson) at the Collège de France in 1900, with implicit 'freedom to teach as he pleased' (Clark, in Tarde, 1969: 7), and whose work was immediately translated into English, indicating perhaps that he was regarded as more successful than Durkheim.

The dramatic nature of the almost diametrical opposition between Tarde and Durkheim became clear in 1893. Tarde's concept of imitation, the basic concept of his whole sociological system, suggested that social regularities, which sociologists might call social structures, were generated out of individual creations (he called them inventions) by processes of imitation and counterimitation. This idea was clearly identified by Durkheim in the *Division* as a conception which 'can explain nothing' (Durkheim, 1964b: 375). Though the dismissal was devastating, Tarde's review of the book as a whole was moderate and even 'generous' (Lukes). Tarde's response was to criticise the work on a number of counts, one of which was to rebuke Durkheim for ignoring the role of the individual genius in the development of the division of labour, indeed for Tarde the division of labour was the effect of the action of individual genius and imitation (Lukes, 1973: 304). In the first chapter of the *Rules* Durkheim specifically notes that imitation is not the basis of the social fact, indeed it 'never expresses what is essential and characteristic of the social fact': it is, in any case, not really a theory but a 'résumé of the immediate data', and theoretically, an individual state impacting on another one remains individual, while the number of ways in which they do impact are so varied even the term leads to possible conceptual confusion (Durkheim, 1982: 59). The criticism struck its target.

Tarde launched his attack on the *Rules* within weeks of its first appearance in print, at the 'First International Congress of Sociology' in Paris in October 1894. In his critique two related questions are posed: what is the nature of the most elementary social phenomenon and what are the elementary social groups? (Tarde, 1969: 113). Tarde discusses the first question through a critique of Durkheim's definition of the social fact. Drawing an analogy with the mechanical action of one body on another, he suggested that the basic fact is simply the action of one human individual consciousness in relation to another. What is social, he maintained, in an act is that part which is communicated between individual consciousnesses, irrespective of any subjective motives which impel them. The common element in this process can be identified as that which individuals imitate from individual to individual. The character of this phenomenon is objective and above all external to the individual's subjective wishes. But, said Tarde, the 'distinguished professor at Bordeaux, M. Durkheim', who otherwise propounds an objective method in sociology objects to this formulation: Durkheim insists that the first characteristic of social facts is that it can be separated from individual manifestations which assumes that social facts can be communicated from the group to the individual. Obviously this is false: they are communicated from individual to individual. To define the sociological object as independent of all individuals, is to 'inject into sociology' a 'veritable scholastic ontology' (1969: 115). Ironically, said Tarde, Durkheim is inconsistent, for the expression adopted in the *Rules*, that collective phenomena are 'passed from mouth to mouth' (Durkheim), means that there is resort to another model, in fact if not in principle (1969: 116). No one who proposes to discuss the social fact *in abstracto* can refer to individual expressions. The social fact as it appears in Durkheim's thought is simply a Platonic Idea, so much so that individual acts which manifest it are not considered to be social at all.

Turning to Durkheim's second characteristic of a social fact, that it is general not because it is repeated but because it is imposed on individuals (an observation specifically aimed at Tarde), Tarde commented: 'At first glance we do not understand.' The error of conceptualisation this time is so gross that it could only have been produced as a purely logical deduction from an already flawed initial definition. It is equivalent to suggesting that what is eminently social is the imposition of regime by fact of conquest, and nothing less social than a 'spontaneous conversion' of a people to a new faith without coercion. But the problem of the externality of social facts to the individual rests on a simple logical error of conception: 'If it can be said that these social things are independent of every one of the members in the sense that if one member disappears the social things do not, is it not because without him their reality is their presence *within* the consciousness or the memory of all the other members?' (1969: 120).

The basic source of this fundamental mistake, said Tarde, is the rather banal idea that emergent properties exist through the combination of lower elements. Social, however, are different from natural physical objects, since in the former we know what the elements are – individuals – and we know that the social is within them. If we go on to say, like Durkheim does, that all explanations by the psychological are false in principle, this appears to mean by implication that 'any clear explanation is necessarily an erroneous one' (1969: 122). Theories which seem also to assume that individuals are 'all identical, all similarly inert' actually present great problems. Indeed, so is the proposition that all social facts should be explained by previous social facts. This would be like trying to argue that 'the determining cause of our railway system should be sought neither in the states of consciousness of Papin, Watts, Stephenson, or others, not in the logical series of ideas and discoveries which dawned on these great minds, but rather in the preexisting network of roads and the parcel post service' (1969: 124). It is necessary to recognise that the term 'social milieu' is empty, and that what exists is a 'constellation' of many individuals – 'some of whom exercise reciprocal influence on each other, and some of whom model themselves on others' (1969: 124–5).

In the following years there were many critical exchanges between Tarde and Durkheim over the formulations in the *Rules* as well as other sociological matters (see Lukes, 1973: 302–313). In an exchange over Durkheim's idea that in every society there exists a normal crime rate, Durkheim accused Tarde (1895, in Durkheim, 1983) of completely misunderstanding his position on virtually every point. The fundamental difference between them, he concluded, was that Tarde reduced 'science to intellectual amusement' and whose ultimate position was 'a more or less consistent mystics (sic) ... the rule of fantasy in the intellectual realm' (Durkheim, 1978: 188). Tarde replied that Durkheim's position which postulated the existence of a normal crime rate was simply an a priori dogma, and that, unlike his own position which did not overrate science, Durkheim's 'anti-mysticism' was far more 'disastrous' than mysticism. Science 'serves all ends, good and bad' he argued (Lukes, 1973: 311).

Durkheim attempted to clarify his position further vis-à-vis Tarde in *Suicide* in a number of analytic comments mainly on the problem of imitative suicide. An entire chapter was devoted to the problem of explanation of suicides by the factor of imitation alone and his conclusions not only clarified the difference between the ideas of individual and social causation, but also of the concept of imitation itself. Three different usages were identified. First, as a term denoting the numerous operations resulting in social harmonies, through the 'reciprocal imitation of each ... by all and of all by each' so that new states are created; secondly, as a term for the 'impulse which drives us to seek harmony with the society to which we belong' and 'we conform solely because (of) social authority'; thirdly, as a notion that we copy or imitate, not because of any intrinsic quality of the action, nor because 'we think it useful, nor to be in harmony with a model' but just because it has occurred. But, he suggests:

It is one thing to share a common feeling, another to yield to the authority of opinion, and a third to repeat automatically what others have done. No reproduction occurs in the first case; in the second it results only from logical operations, judgments and reasonings, implicit or explicit, but themselves the essence of the phenomenon; and thus reproduction cannot be the definition. It becomes all embracing only in the third case. There it is all-comprehensive; the new act is a mere echo of the original. Nor does it repeat, but this repetition has no cause for existence outside itself, only the total of characteristics which make us imitative creatures under certain circumstances. The name of imitation must then be reserved solely for such facts if it is to have clear meaning, and we shall say: *Imitation exists when the immediate antecedent of an act is the representation of a like act, previously performed by someone else; with no explicit mental operation which bears upon the intrinsic nature of the act reproduced intervening between representation and execution* (1970: 129).

Durkheim here had identified a central problem in Tarde's position but had not really grasped his analysis completely, for Tarde had written that the process moves:

from *within* to *without*, if we try to express it more precisely, (it) means two things: 1. that imitation of ideas precedes the imitation of their expression. 2. that imitation of ends precedes imitation of means. Ends or ideas are the *inner things*, means or expressions, the outer. (Tarde, (1888) 1903: 207).

In other words, say with respect to the development of language, that: 'if the listener merely repeated (the) sound like a parrot ... it is impossible to see how this superficial and mechanical *re-echoing* could have led him to understand' (1903:204). Thus Tarde suggests not simply the imitation of the act but a necessary prior imitation of the 'meaning'. The problem is in some cases, he suggested, that 'women and children' do only imitate the outside and not the inside of an action.

A number of further critical exchanges occurred after this, and in 1903 they met to debate the relation of sociology to the social sciences. Durkheim outlined his conception of sociology again. Tarde replied that the study of social facts can only be about 'acts relevant to inter-mental psychology' (Tarde, 1969:138). The use of a comparative method without this fundamental orientation is a 'waste of time'. As inter-mental psychology is the elemental fact of social life it is in itself 'general' to all the social sciences and 'thanks to it sociology can be a central science' (1969:139).

Durkheim replied:

> M. Tarde claims that sociology will arrive at such and such results; but in the present state of our knowledge we cannot say what the elementary social fact is.... Whatever this inter-mental psychology is worth, it is inadmissible for it to exercise a sort of directive action on the special disciplines of which it must be the product. (1969:140)

Tarde replied: 'I understand your methodology which is pure ontology.... There can only be individual actions and interactions. The rest is only a metaphysical entity, mysticism.' (1969:140)

Durkheim reviewed Tarde's essay 'L'Interpsychologie' in L'Année of 1906, which stressed again his view that Tarde's ideas revolved in a 'vicious circle': it 'presupposes what it produces' (Durkheim, 1980:72–3). Although Tarde had died in 1904, his son carried on the battle against the 'family enemy' (Clark, 1973:193). Under the pseudonym 'Agathon' he charged Durkheim in 1911 of having established at the Sorbonne an 'intellectual despotism ... (and) has made of his teaching an instrument of domination' (cited by Clark, 1973:193). What particularly pained Guillaume de Tarde was that Durkheim's course on pedagogy was the only obligatory course for all students of the agrégation, 'and those who miss two or three lectures are not permitted to pass exams'.

The debate between Durkheim and Tarde was complicated by personal animosity, and this certainly affected Durkheim's arguments, as can best be seen perhaps in the difference between his replies to Tarde and his considerations of Tardean arguments presented by others. One clear case of this is his review of the work of E. A. Ross who developed an influential Tardean social psychology in America. In 1901 Durkheim noted in a review that Ross's arguments (that moral revolutions are the work of individual geniuses, who are able to see their pro-social ideas accepted because individuals hypocritically repress their anti-social feelings) 'begs the question' since 'shame in expressing immoral sentiments, by which we intend to explain the authority of moral ideas is by itself a consequence and another aspect of this authority'. But he concluded 'it remains to be said that the article has merit since it draws our attention to a very much neglected subject which is completely fundamental' (Durkheim, 1980: 120–1).

SIMON DEPLOIGE

Deploige's book, *The Conflict between Ethics and Sociology*, which appeared in France in 1911, undertook a full examination and critique of Durkheim's sociology. Deploige examined its antecedents and particularly its claims to be able to point the way to a new conception of moral life which might transcend traditional Catholicism. Written with considerable passion and partisanship, there is contained here, not only an attempt to show that all of Durkheim's main ideas were imported into France from Germany, but they can be traced to an obscure early nineteenth-century writer called Adam Müller (Deploige, 1938: 167). The work contains besides this a philosophical and logical critique of the *Rules*.

Deploige presented a very full summary of Durkheim's orientations in sociology and suggests there are seven essential 'steps' to his methodology: 1. adopt the attitude of Cartesian doubt; 2. take a group of social phenomena which manifest common external characteristics defined in advance; 3. approach these from an aspect from which they can be examined in isolation from their individual manifestations; 4. explanation must be solely sociological; 5. proofs of sociological analysis must use the method of concomitant variations; 6. full analysis must show how the social fact 'has been progressively composed'; 7. the approach to the analysis of any one social fact requires an elaboration of the classification of the main social types (Deploige, 1938: 48–80). After presenting the *Rules*, Deploige subjects it to thorough criticism: the definition of the social fact proceeds not in relation to anything that exists but as a dialectical artifice – it is deduced from a theoretical postulate that society is reality in its own right, but the idea that morality exists as rules of sanctioned conduct which also impose themselves on the individual is simply 'the fruit of a hasty induction' (1938: 37). The discussion of this induction in the *Rules* is full of contradictions: his classification of society starts from the pure notion of the 'horde' rather than any thing; his discussion of the family is not functional for he 'suddenly transports himself to the very sources of evolution' in the Comtean manner (1938: 363). Durkheim's discussion of proofs is vitiated since he argues that the method proceeds purely through comparisons but then a supplementary 'interpretation' has to be done. Deploige continues at length, and concludes:

> It is true that we find elsewhere almost all the rules of the sociological method ... but these borrowings, sorted and moulded, arranged and grouped, make a rather coherent group. ... But the consistency which these rules seem to possess in the ideal order, where they sustain one another, only masks their fragility ... (1938: 358–9)
>
> The instrument was not constructed little by little by an artisan in the course of repeated trials that would have enabled him to test the solidity of each part and of the whole. It was fabricated by a dialectician according to his subjective and arbitrary preconception of social things.... (1938: 367)

The central problem is that the conceptualisation is disputed by historians and their charge is that Durkheim has illegitimately inserted theory into the definitions and therefore into the very methodological rules, which are not independent of doctrine as Durkheim claims. Consequently, Durkheim is not really a social scientist at all but a moralist selling his wares in a secular form. Deploige concludes simply by reaffirming the Catholic faith and calling on sociologists to read the works of St Thomas.

Durkheim had commented in 1907 on parts of Deploige's characterisations when they were published in advance of the book. He specifically questioned the accuracy of the reduction of argument that all the major ideas were German in origin, particularly to some of the works mentioned which he had never read. His 'social realism' was influenced in the main by Comte, Spencer and Espinas, and the difference between sociology and psychology was stressed by his teacher Boutroux, who cited Aristotle. It was accepted by Comte. The main influence on his conception of the sociology of religion was Robertson Smith and the English school. 'My aim' he said, 'has been precisely to introduce that idea [sociology] into disciplines from which it was absent and thereby to make them branches of sociology' (Durkheim, 1982: 257–60).

In the *Année* of 1913 Durkheim wrote a very brief review of this long book, saying that his only reason for commenting was to 'denounce the polemical arguments' deployed against him. Again Durkheim stressed the fact that his ideas could not be called Germanic, but this time he appealed also to the influence on his work of Renouvier (Durkheim, 1980: 160). Out of the mass of argumentation and substantiation Durkheim picked out a misquotation by Deploige from an article by Durkheim of 1898. Durkheim gave the two side by side and comments 'there is no timidity about resorting to a *conscious alteration of the texts*.... The readers will judge for themselves' (1980: 160).

CHARLES SEIGNOBOS

Seignobos wrote a number of works on historical methodology, one of which, *La Méthode Historique Appliquée aux Sciences Sociales* (1901), appeared to attack Durkheim's sociological method directly. His argument began by discussing the theory of the document and its prerequisites – a study of writing, language, thought, belief, knowledge and the links between these 'necessary operations' and 'reality'. In order for there to be critical understanding of these processes there has to be evolved a critique of the juridical conception of the witness, and this entails a theory of interpretation. The status of facts in the social sciences is particularly problematic. There cannot be an entirely objective methodology since the nature of social reality is essentially subjective. At this point in his discussion he asks: do collective acts belong to the same species as individual acts? (1901: 107). 'It is', he says, 'a controversial question, but a philosophical question, indifferent to the application of method'. It is against the scientific spirit to assume that there are a priori characteristics in the thing studied. But each human act is always motivated and one can always give two interpretations to such acts: one is psychological and relates to the will, the other is physiological and relates to drives. In the social sciences the subject matter must be related to human consciousness and so there must be recourse to psychology. The idea of trying to study external facts separately from internal motives would be like trying to 'understand the movements of an orchestra without knowing the music they play' (1901: 109).

Durkheim reviewed this book in 1902. The idea, he says, seems to be that social science like history can never be more than a conjectural approximation of subjective construction. Either the social sciences are consigned to be a branch history or they are denied a right to exist. This arbitrarily narrows the range of the social sciences – why not tolerate comparative law, criminology, political geography, the science of religions, and sociology? These subjects all use objective methods that go beyond the use of a subjective documentary method. The comparative method exists, and psychology has been successful using objective methods.

Seignobos and Durkheim met in debate over methodology in 1908. Seignobos seemed very much on the defensive, denying all validity to the search for laws in history and the use of the comparative method to discover them. 'So' asked Durkheim, 'what the historian really arrives at are the conscious causes? And everything else remains a closed book ...?' 'Not entirely a closed book' replied Seignobos, 'but more so than what is conscious.' 'So the causes which are most immediately available to the historian are the inner motives, such as they appear to the participants?' Durkheim queried. 'Why do they enjoy this privileged position?' he continued. 'But that's very simple', said Seignobos, 'because the participants and witnesses afford us an explanation of the conscious acts.' Durkheim seemed to regard this as an astonishing limitation on the historical imagination. (Durkheim, 1982: 211–28).

ALFRED FOUILLÉE

Fouillée wrote widely and ambitiously on sociological issues and in many respects seemed close to Durkheim, even dedicating his work *Les Eléments Sociologiques de la Morale* (1905) to him. Fouillée was also one of the contributors to the international symposium on Durkheim's paper concerning sociology and the social sciences in London in 1904. He explained there his concern with a sociology which conceives

society as something which is not merely the medium in which things happen, not merely the environment and theatre for the play of individual actions, but as itself an actor or agent, and an agent which consciously reacts back on itself (in Galton et al., 1905: 230)

But in this contribution Fouillée judiciously avoided criticising Durkheim as he had done elsewhere for his objectivist tendencies. When Durkheim came to review these criticisms in 1907 he began by suggesting that Fouillée had a 'very peculiar idea of the method we practise and of the goal we pursue'. He tried to dispel the idea that his writings had suggested that sociology could only describe (not analyse) and that the problem of value judgments had been avoided in the search for purely objective causes.

Had this been the totality of the dispute it would be of little significance, but what made it interesting was Fouillée's suggestion that if Durkheim's objective was to establish some sort of moral system there was no need to make long and detailed investigations since the elements of basic morality are known by everyone. 'The real service rendered by Fouillée's criticism is to have openly admitted this surprising assumption,' said Durkheim (1980: 141). The problem of the apparent simplicity of 'the ideas, the sentiments, that the rules of conduct express . . . – as the "me" appears a simple matter for introspection – are in reality the resultants at times of very numerous components . . .' (1980: 141–2). What is often assumed in order to support these oversimplified notions is the idea that there is a single human nature that can be relied on to explain social forms. Clearly moral structures vary considerably, and this is apparent without any recourse to sociology. Durkheim then introduces a very surprising argument:

What is first and foremost . . . is to dissipate the prejudice according to which morality would appear to be a system of truisms; it is essential to convey the extreme complexity of the ideas and feelings of which morality is the result. At present, there is no doubt that this complexity is much more fully sensed and understood when it is recognised that moral practices are social institutions, placed under the domination of social factors . . . it does not follow a priori that all moral life is necessarily, entirely expressible in sociological terms . . . we only want to assert that this individual and inner side is neither the whole nor even the essential element. (1980: 143)

Durkheim returned to this argument in 1917, the last year of his life, when he was working on his *Ethics* for Fouillée's assertion was quoted prominently as the position against which Durkheim's whole sociology was aimed to displace (Durkheim, 1979: 84, 87).

GEORGES SOREL

Sorel's long 1895 review of the *Rules* sought to show how close Durkheim was to the materialist position of the Marxists. He suggested that Durkheim's conception of method was a genuine effort and aimed at valid objectives, despite its flawed positions on certain points. He added to Durkheim's own comparisons the suggestion that sociology is rather like meteorology: both are interested in large scale movements of masses, currents, etc., both have recourse to the analysis of frequencies and regularities and both are aimed at practical objectives. Durkheim, however, had a tendency to define the object of sociology as having essential elements, a thing in itself, not as a relationship. This tendency was evident also in his definition of the social milieu. No one, however, would want to speak of a 'planetary milieu' but of a system of relationships, for 'they do not form a more or less homogeneous melange' (Sorel, 1895: ii, 149). But it is clear, he said, that Marx also shows that political, religious, and cultural systems are connected with an infrastructure (153). If Marx had indeed shown that the categories of bourgeois society are not eternal, what mode of reason can be adopted in order to analyse the changes in these categories? It has to be critical, Sorel suggested, and this means socialist: a non-socialist sociology is incapable of analysing the way that the division of labour is related to the class struggle. Taking a move in this direction would give Durkheim a support against the purely logical nature of his sociology. Against the trend of many other critics, Sorel thought there was still a trace of the psychological element in Durkheim's notion of the social fact and that this should be eliminated. Sorel concluded that 'no thinker is as well prepared as he to introduce the theories of Karl Marx into higher education' (1895: ii, 180). This of course was not to happen and Sorel was astonished at Durkheim's development. In his *Reflections on Violence* he noted that Durkheim came to regard the religious element in ethics as supremely important and cited this to show 'to what point the character of the sublime impresses itself on authors who, by the nature of their work, would seem the least inclined to accept it' (Sorel, 1961: 207).

Durkheim did not write a specific reply to this invitation. To the conclusion of the *Rules* he added a note in 1895 emphasising how inappropriate it was 'to characterise our method as materialist', a position he was to sustain throughout his career.

9

French Discussion of the *Rules* After 1917

Analysis and discussion of the *Rules* in France after 1917 was wide ranging. When Lévi-Strauss came to survey the results of the first half century of French sociology in 1945 he concluded that the overwhelming influence for both good and bad had been Durkheimian. Before looking at the critique of Durkheim contained in this survey, it is worth examining the outstanding effort of 1920s to assess the *Rules* – that by Roger Lacombe.

In his *La Méthode Sociologique de Durkheim* Lacombe attempted a detailed assessment of Durkheim's project, and the essay has been extremely influential. His conclusions were that Durkheim had made a radical and ambitious 'synthesis' of significant philosophical currents with the empirical social sciences, so that the true originality of Durkheim lay in the ideal of sociology as a single science encompassing all the social disciplines, with the primary emphasis on experimental and positive research aimed at producing sociological laws through the constant interrogation of facts (Lacombe, 1926: 13–4). The main problem was that this project was in danger; it needed to be defended against the specialists and the philosophers. There were some elements in Durkheim's own formulations which might lead to the project being rejected for entirely spurious reasons. Particularly weak was Durkheim's conceptualisation of the *conscience collective*, which was in some respects a purely arbitrary hypothesis, open to the charge of sociological anthropomorphism (1926: 38). Linked to this was a seriously ambiguous conceptualisation of social facts themselves defined in terms of 'constraint' which was used in at least three different ways: the term should be rejected (1926: 42–8). It was still possible, however, to find a completely acceptable definition even within the *Rules* themselves: a social fact is any way of acting which has an existence in society independent of its individual manifestations. Usage of this concept in *Suicide* confirms this possibility. It maintains, against Tarde and the positivist tradition of Comte and Spencer, the idea of causation specifically linked to social species, and it is this which is essential to Durkheim's sociology, and is its radical element (1926: 52).

The unfortunate intrusion of the definition of social facts by the characteristic of constraint is related to a constant philosophical pre-occupation, which culminated in the equation of society = god. This emphasis is at root a moralism, but it found its way into the initial sociological definitions through the link of constraint with moral duty, and thus into the concept of the *conscience collective* and into the analysis of the social categories in the sociology of knowledge. If Durkheim was able to identify the essence of religion as the *conscience* of society itself this resolves the investigation into an elaboration of an already known phenomenon, something that Durkheim had charged against Tarde over the concept of imitation. It is thus a deviation from Durkheim's own principles. But as Durkheim came to concentrate on the sociology of religion with this definition already in hand, sociology was displaced by philosophical interpretation. In order for sociology to return to its major task it has to be clearly separated from phil-osophy – and in Durkheimian sociology this means that the concept of the *conscience collective* must be abandoned altogether (1926: 66).

Lacombe thought that Durkheim's conception of the process of formulation of initial definitions was also seriously defective. Far from being able to remove preconceptions, Durkheim introduced pre-conceptions a priori into the definitions; this is only a non-scientific form if these initial definitions are regarded as other than provisional (1926: 108–9). This is also true of the basic problem of the classification of social types, which, far from being the product of serious theoretical and empirical work, appears easily solved in the *Rules*, again a priori. In fact, Durkheim's definition of the social species is apparently able to intervene in order to specify that feudal society is not a social species by reference to the essential characteristic of species rather than approaching the classification through a knowledge of actual species. This is an inappropriate way in which to use the biological analogy, as is Durkheim's use of the medical model to solve the question of the definition of social goals. The idea of health as the norm, *par excel-*

lence, does not set up true moral imperatives, since the specifications are subordinate to an already given acceptance of an end, which science does not itself impose but which is determined by our own will (1926: 135). And when Durkheim talks of the abnormal there is a confusion of the exceptional and the pathological which it is essential to distinguish between, particularly as regards practice (1926: 140). Lacombe concludes that these errors can indeed be rectified but on condition that the sociological enterprise disassociates itself from philosophical concerns, and in consequence assumes a more modest stance in the analysis of social facts divested of the burden of the metaphysical concept of the *conscience collective.*

When Lévi-Strauss came to review the social sciences in France in 1945 he suggested that Durkheim's influence was dominant not only in sociology but as far afield as psychology, history, economics, law and linguistics, and he even noted an encounter between Durkheimian sociologists (e.g. Roger Caillois) and surrealists (e.g. Bataille), in the short-lived Collège de Sociologie at the end of the 1930s. Having surveyed these developments he turned to a critique of some of the weaknesses of Durkheimian methodology as he saw it. His main charge was levelled at the theory of symbolism in the *Elementary Forms,* which he judged full of contradictions and violent oscillations of position. Durkheim, in his definition of 'elementary forms', confuses the historical and the logical modes of analysis, a theoretical confusion which gives rise to oscillations between the two poles in analysis as the fundamental dualism of methodology is exposed (Lévi-Strauss 1945: 517). This is revealed in the *Elementary Forms* in the way that Durkheim is caught when trying to account for symbolism in society. On the one hand he suggests that society is unthinkable without symbolism (or virtually), but when symbolism has to be explained the argument becomes genetic: he tries to deduce the symbol from representation, and the emblem from experience (1945: 518) in a vicious circle. This is ultimately related to an inconsistency: on the one hand the social is regarded as a hierarchy of levels, some of which are intermediaries, but on the other the distinction between the individual and the social is absolute. Further, because Durkheim conceived the existence of only one type of teleology, a conscious type, and insisted in removing virtually all teleology from sociological explanation, he failed to find an answer to his own most basic question: 'how social phenomena may present the character of being meaningful wholes' (1945: 520), not for any lack of insight but simply because the means of solving the methodological question, to be found in linguistics and psychology, had not yet been produced. The basic conclusion: Durkheim's sociology oscillated between 'a dull empiricism and an aprioristic frenzy' (1945: 528); Marcel Mauss, however, had demonstrated that it was possible to find ways of escaping from this polarity by curtailing the methodology at key points so as to reduce its philosophical and evolutionist ambitions. Lévi-Strauss even proposed a rapprochement with the work of Tarde whose work was 'almost forgotten'.

The criticism of Durkheim's conception of the *conscience collective* was also made in a major examination by Georges Gurvitch which tried to present a systematic conception of the main elements of Durkheim's conception of social structure. The basic theory of social symbolism was its reliance on the contradictory assertions that symbols both express social solidarity and produce it (Gurvitch 1950: 359). The problem stems from the acceptance of a dogmatic prejudgment in the definition of the idea of the *conscience collective* as an emergent phenomenon imposed on individuals from without. First, this appeared as suggesting that the collective *conscience* was identical with individual *conscience*; second, in the *Rules* that it was an external constraint; third, as a transcendental imperativity; fourth, as preexisting and possessing greater richness than the individual *conscience*; fifth, suggesting fundamental discontinuities between the collective and the individual; but also sixth, the idea that the *conscience collective* engenders duties; seventh, that it engenders ideals; eighth, that a logical universality is incarnated through the *conscience collective*; and finally that this *conscience* merges with the divine (1950: 407). Gurvitch suggests that this development reveals the intrusion of an ambiguity so that Durkheim 'oscillates' between a view of a 'collective subjectivism' and a 'metaphysics of the Spirit' (1950: 361–2), or is permanently tempted by the view of the *conscience collective* as harmonious, unified, as a Logos, modelled on Comte's 'Grand Being of Humanity' or Hegel's 'Objective Spirit' (1950: 404). The *Rules* are interpreted in this analysis as offering specifically new arguments for this objective idealism, especially those concerned with the characteristics of externality and constraint (1950: 369–373). The development of sociology, however, requires the ejection of this concept from its vocabulary.

The major work of the 1960s was Guy Aimard's *Durkheim et la Science Economique,* which presented a long sympathetic discussion of Durkheim's methodology. Defined as realist, recognising that Durkheim himself specifically guarded against hypostatising social phenomena, his method is found to be coherent, overcoming most of the central difficulties encountered by subjectivist and formalist sociology (Tarde, Simmel and Weber). It is essentially experimental and undogmatic. There is, however, a specific shift from the materialist and dialectical early works to a later position which appears to combine Kant and Comte in a perspective which is 'hyperspiritualist' (Durkheim). Sociology, if it is to be successful, must purge these philosophical intrusions and return to the firm ground of social science. He specifically compared the propositions at the conclusion of the *Rules* which suggest that sociology must remain independent of philosophy, with the position reached in 1909 which suggests that sociology contribute to the renewal of philosophy (Aimard, 1962: 235).

Of more recent essays, the works of Jean-Claude Filloux and Bernard Lacroix are representative, and both reveal a shift of emphasis. Filloux suggests that the fundamental originality of Durkheim, methodologically, is to have proposed a new articulation of the problematic of efficient cause and teleology, with that of expressive social causation (Filloux, 1977: 101). Certainly, he says, there is an ambiguity of terminology at certain points, but Durkheim's use of the biological analogy to suggest both the necessity of structure and system on the one hand and morphology and function on the other produces a complex epistemological structure: when the social structures are identified as expressions or manifestations of currents of opinion they are nevertheless stratified and posed in a form where the question of the determinant milieu can be raised. This seems to suggest that Durkheim thinks of society as a complex overdetermined structure (1977: 122). Whereas Marx proposed a conception of society as emanating from an economic base and in which there is class contradiction, Durkheim saw social structure as emanating from currents of thought in which social discrepancies arise through social malintegration. In this body of thought the *Rules* is a key statement of this complexity (1977, Ch. 3).

Bernard Lacroix, in his *Durkheim et le Politique* (1981) argues that Durkheim's work is not characterised by continuity, but that there is an epistemological 'break' which can be dated around the year 1895. Before this turning point Durkheim's work is above all dominated by a rigorous and all-embracing determinism. The *Rules* is an intermediate work which does still maintain that morphology is preponderant, but 'very quickly follows other formulas which anticipate, irresistibly, the

Elementary Forms': the active factor becomes the specifically human milieu and this displaces the emphasis, in the *Division*, on material density. There is a direct criticism in the *Rules* of the formulation of the idea that moral density is an expression of material density. The *Rules* also admits that first causes in the absolute sense of the word are not permitted in science, a position repeated in 1912. But what is most evident is the way in which the *Rules* inverts key formulas of the *Division*; in the *Rules* we find:

> The determining cause of a social fact must be sought among antecedent social facts and not among the states of the individual consciousness. (Durkheim, 1982: 134)

> The primary origin of social processes of any importance must be sought in the constitution of the inner social environment. (1982: 135)

These must be compared, says Lacroix, with Durkheim's position in *Division*:

> The determining cause of a social fact must be sought [in the constitution of the inner social environment] and not among the states of the individual consciousness. (Lacroix, 1981: 121)

> The primary origin of social processes of any importance must be sought [among the antecedent social facts]. (1981: 121)

Lacroix suggests that the *Rules* is an extraordinary inversion of the formulations of the earlier work which shift the primary emphasis from the material milieu to the human milieu. The later works continue this movement towards a voluntarism which becomes more and more pronounced (1981: 106). (It should be noted that the second set of 'quotations' have been constructed by Lacroix himself out of Durkheim's sentence in the *Division*: 'it is in certain variations of the social environment that we must seek the cause that explains the progress of the division of labour' (Durkheim, 1984: 200). And that analysis has thus been charged with a certain freedom!)

10

The Anglo-Saxon Reception of the *Rules*

DURING DURKHEIM'S LIFETIME

The reception of the *Rules* in America was overwhelmingly hostile. The work was first fully summarised and discussed in a review of French sociology in the *American Journal of Sociology* in 1896, by J. H. Tufts. In January 1898 Gustavo Tosti followed this up by contributing a critical essay on 'Suicide in the light of recent studies' which considered Durkheim's wider methodological position. Durkheim himself was stung to reply, making one of his rare and almost invariably ineffective sorties into the Anglo-Saxon orbit. He accused Tosti of making some fundamental errors of interpretation, especially concerning his conception of the relation of the individual to society. In July of that year Tosti answered these criticisms in an extremely hostile essay entitled 'The delusions of Durkheim's sociological objectivism'. He insisted that Durkheim had ignored the contribution of the individual to the construction of social phenomena. Without this element, he wrote, 'the cyclopic scaffolding of a so-called "objective" sociology falls into ruins, and nothing is left of it but a certain number of vague and empty formulas' (Tosti, 1898: 176). Durkheim left it there. These articles initiate in the Anglo-Saxon world a parallel to what had already become a mainly acrimonious and negative reception in France itself. The persistent line of criticism followed the objection that Durkheim was utterly mistaken to suggest that social phenomena are external to the individual and above all must be analysed by using a method which avoided the subjectivity of the individual. Such an approach appeared to be an obstacle to the development of sociology. Tarde's own sociological orientation seemed much more reasonable to the Americans, and his *Social Laws* and *Laws of Imitation* were translated in 1899 and 1903. Durkheim had to wait until 1915 for a major work to appear in English translation.

Durkheim's conception of the nature of sociology and its relation to the other social sciences was debated in England under the auspices of the Sociological Society in London in 1904. The debate was published in 1905 along with written contributions from many continental scholars. Durkheim's sociological orientations received some support but a large number of the contributors were critical: the publication made available in English the criticisms of French sociologists such as Marcel Bernès and Alfred Fouillée. More generally, sociologists in Britain showed little interest in the *Rules*, whereas anthropologists entered into a number of critical debates. Durkheim reviewed Andrew Lang's *Social Origins* in 1903. Lang replied with a direct attack on Durkheim's theory of totemism as self-contradictory. Durkheim this time replied saying that Lang had extracted propositions out of context. The highly influential anthropologist Radcliffe-Brown noted in an analysis of 1913 that his own examination of the Australian kinship system seemed to suggest that Durkheim's analyses were empirically incorrect (Radcliffe-Brown, 1913: 193). He sent a copy to Durkheim. Durkheim replied in 1913 by letter (published in Durkheim et al., 1960: 317–18), in which he stressed that he was pleased to see that they were in agreement on method 'nothing could have given me greater confidence in the method I am trying to apply'. Radcliffe-Brown was later to write in 1938, that the *Rules* was the first major statement of 'structural-functionalism' as a method.

One book, however, can be taken to sum up the prevailing assessment of Durkheim's work amongst Anglo-Saxon sociologists in the pre-war period, Charles Gehlke's *Emile Durkheim's Contributions to Sociological Theory* of 1915. Like Barnes' immediately post-war essay (Barnes, 1920), Gehlke stresses Durkheim's specific brand of guild socialism, but notes an apparent affinity with Kropotkin's anarchism, yet in this case tinged with a flavour of social compromise ('syndicat ouvrier-patroniste'). The central discussion was focused squarely on the significance of the theoretical premisses of Durkheim's method (Gehlke, 1915: 126–49). After a lengthy summary, he supported the main charges against Durkheim made by Tarde, Tosti and others, but adds that these critiques do not really get to the root of the problem –

not Durkheim's conclusions but their 'logical premisses' (1915: 94). Only at one point does Gehlke really disagree with the general line of criticism: Durkheim should not be understood as a crude 'realist' since, he said, some of Durkheim's arguments on the nature of social reality seem compatible with the views of Bergson and William James (1915: 84–92). Durkheim's whole theoretical system rests on mistaken premisses: it is 'metaphysical' (94), 'intellectualist' (96), reduces the psychological to the biological (97), but above all ignores the role of the individual as an active cause of social phenomena. The sociologist should start frankly from the starting point of the existing purely individual mind (1915: 101). Gehlke then himself proceeded to construct a synthesis out of the conceptions of Le Bon, Tarde, McDougall, Giddings, Baldwin, Cooley and Ross. This alternative is so successful, he suggests, that it is clear sociology must abandon Durkheim. He sums up his position:

> Our minds, as individual members of a group of associating minds, are in constant interaction; each mind is a function of all the others. There is thus a basic oneness in diversity. Out of this socially produced oneness ... springs, in reaction to common stimulation, a like response ... the process eventuates, on its functional side, in a uniformity of action consciously perceived and directed by the agents, with a value heightened, by reason of the magnitude of the reciprocal processes involved, far beyond the limits of the value of the purely individual act.... These social types of action acquire an emotion-tone, and a volitional force ... which set them apart from the specifically individual actions. (1915: 105–6)

AFTER 1917

The ways in which Durkheim's work was being assessed by the end of the 1930s in Britain and America were in many ways strikingly different from those of the earlier period. The emerging world crisis and the reaction to it in the Anglo-Saxon social sciences led to a climate in which it was widely argued that Durkheim's sociology was implicated in the rise of totalitarianism. Certain left-wing factions of Italian fascism had flirted with Durkheimian sociology in the 1920s, just as Sorel had done before 1914. Thus when the first English translation of the *Rules* appeared in 1938 it was introduced by George Catlin as a work of purely metaphysical inspiration which, in part, contributed to the rise of fascism. Not only this but the work was very badly written, was full of 'laboured platitudes', and undertook the 'deplorable effort' of attempting to interpret social phenomena in terms of the collective consciousness. He admitted, however, that the concept of the social fact was of 'high significance in detecting the essentials of sound method' but was 'defective in precision' in Durkheim's hands. The work was also flawed in its evolutionism and conflation of science and ethics.

There were signs that at the end of the 1930s a more serious examination of Durkheim was underway. Here I take two essays from those years, by Alpert and Parsons, to illustrate this. Although Alpert's appeared slightly later than that of Parsons, his treatment was the more traditional of the two. He presented Durkheim's method as an analytical schema composed of seven steps: 1. define the problem; 2. criticise existing theories; 3. tentatively posit causal relations; 4. place the causal nexus in an axiological system; 5. establish operative secondary factors; 6. treat these as in 4, and 7. derive the theoretical consequences of these (Alpert, 1939: 95–7). Alpert deduces these not only from the *Rules* but also from Durkheim's actual practice. In a brief examination of one essay, on the causes of the First World War, Alpert argues that Durkheim adopts a subjective approach similar to that of Max Weber. But Alpert viewed the *Rules* as the major statement of 'objectivism' in sociological writing, and on this his conclusions were extremely hostile to Durkheim's ideas: the 'specific rules ... are shackles' from which contemporary sociology should, by all the means at its disposal, attempt to liberate itself. For as he has shown, even Durkheim 'freed himself from them' (1939: 127), and his actual method is quite different from those he advocated.

This attack on the *Rules* was sustained by arguing that even if Durkheim's general aims were 'laudable' his conception of the role of definitions in sociology was 'erroneous and constitutes one of the weakest parts of his methodology' (1939: 114). This is because the role of the definer is never brought into the discussion. Things appear to define themselves. Alpert flatly denied that the assertion that the standpoint of the sociologist should be that of an objective recognition of the externality of the social fact is anything but 'illusory and impossible' (1939: 116). There was, he said, a deceptive circle of reasoning here: we must study social things which appear most object-like, yet this rests on an unargued assumption about what object-like is. The method also failed to specify how a class of objects is to be delimited, so this is left to an arbitrary practice of sociologists. Definitions which make their appearance in Durkheim's work appeared to be rigid and dogmatic assertions which fix the discussion to a certain course; they should, in a more adequate method, act like guide posts to investigation. Durkheim's recommendation that phenomena should be studied in a form which most clearly separates them from individual manifestations likewise 'imposes on sociology a totally unwarranted limitation on its effective data' (1939: 125). Bayet's study of suicide was superior to that of Durkheim's because it used a more subtle mode of investigation, and was open to a richer array of sources.

Finally, Alpert turned to the questions of Durkheim's alleged social realism. Many of the problems here, he suggested, are of Durkheim's own making since his terminology was confused and inadequate. Part of the problem arose because of a grave tactical error. Durkheim was too prone to challenge his opponents on their ground, with the consequence that he made too many theoretical concessions. An essential clarification of what Durkheim was for and what he was against is required. Durkheim seemed prepared to accept the existence of individuals as beings who could be thought of as separate from society and exist entirely in their own right, for polemical reasons, in his effort to criticise utilitarianism from a sociological point of view. But his own attitude to the individual was clearly in opposition to this concession. In fact, Alpert suggested, it is very likely that Durkheim believed that society was not an ontological being with its own sense apparatus. On the other hand he was not a nominalist. A third possibility exists. Alpert calls this relational realism: the postulation of a society as a network of relationships, not as a transcendental entity. The criticism of Durkheim which resulted in the question 'where does society exist if not in individuals?' overlooked the possibility that there are levels of phenomena here, and that it was quite possible to think of individuals as a specific substratum of a network of relationships. This is, after all, said Alpert, merely what has already been suggested in the work of Perry and Cooley in America.

The other major work of this period which may be taken for discussion, that of Talcott Parsons, may be said to be the most important contribution to the debate and to raising the status of Durkheim's work written in English. The long meditation on Durkheim's development contained in *The Structure of Social Action* tried to outline a remarkable theoretical evolution, an epistemological maturation in which his project moved from an early simple positivistic orientation to a complex voluntarism. Like Alpert, Parsons too stressed the correction to the idea that Durkheim's thought was built on the premiss of the ontological superiority of a group-mind over the individual.

'To the great majority of sociologists Durkheim is still . . . the leading holder of the "unsound" "group-mind" theory. It would be difficult to discover a more striking example of the way in which preconceived conceptual schemes can prevent the dissemination of important ideas' (Parsons, 1937: 463). The *Rules* is situated in the process of Durkheim's evolving theory as an early synthesis growing out of a critique of the positivism of *The Division of Labour in Society* of 1893. Durkheim's work then entered a period of transition beginning around 1898 which led to a 'new general' position established fully by 1912. This late synthesis was established in the debris of the complete breakdown of the positivist framework itself (1937: 305). The fact that there were different kinds of work produced by Durkheim meant that no overall condemnation and rejection could be valid.

Parsons argued that Durkheim's early work was a sustained attack on the fundamental assumptions of utilitarianism using a number of specifically positivist methods, key elements of which were the stress on the externality of the social world to the actor, and that social facts are neutral and resistant. This does not mean Durkheim is a realist. He was, said Parsons, a radical positivist. The decisive moment in his development came with the recognition of the limitations of the purely negative definition of the social fact in relation to the individual actor. The conception of the social fact was simply too broad, embracing physical, biological and psychological elements. Social facts, the central object of discussion, seemed in many ways extra-social in the early conceptualisation, a problem which Durkheim began to tackle as an empirical problem after 1898. Social facts were then treated more as relational and psychological phenomena. This raised the problem of the mode of determination of non-social facts, and the ways in which this might be represented. Even if the analysis of social facts was based on a recognition of their psychic elements, it remained to be discovered in what specific ways they were social. Durkheim's attention moved towards the analysis of belief systems analysed as cognitive systems. The 'group mind' idea, then, was perhaps only an initial conjecture, a product of the early attempts to pose the problem of the nature of social reality. The *Rules* could not have been written when these problems had been reorganised after 1898, though Durkheim never completely abandoned some of the earlier terminology.

It is clear then from the major discussions at the end of this period, at least in sociology, that the *Rules* had been rejected as an adequate statement of sociological method, though it had now become clear that it was a major reference point for discourse on method, one that was defective, extreme, and was either never used (Alpert) by its creator or was abandoned (Parsons) by him.

For two decades after the war, Anglo-Saxon sociology was dominated by the methodological consensus of structural-functionalism supplemented by an interactionist social psychology. The sources for this were the success of functionalism in anthropology, which some have traced back to Durkheim's influence, and the development of the research programmes of Parsons, Merton, Kingsley Davis, Nisbet, Shils, Warner and others in the USA. (For a direct discussion see Pope et al., 1975; Marshall, 1975). Much of the writing of this neo-Durkheimianism, even when it was concerned with outlining a specifically functionalist methodology, did not claim adherence directly to the *Rules*. There were few attempts to expound or criticise Durkheim's methodology explicitly. Nisbet's essays are perhaps an exception, but there is no doubt that he thought that the *Rules* had suffered unduly from the persistence of grave misconceptions perhaps arising out of the way that Durkheim had been interpreted before the work became available in English. He tried to remedy this by arguing that the work was one of the most profound essays on method in the social sciences (1975: 33). One essay of the 1950s (Gisbert, 1959) can be taken here as illustrating at least one type of criticism which was current in that period.

Gisbert's essay at least has the merit of suggesting that it is representative on one main point:

> In more than twenty years experience as a student and teacher of sociology in various countries, I have never come across a person who ... did not interpret him ... in a quasi-idealistic way as deifying society and making of it an autonomous reality external and superior to individuals. (1959: 358–9)

According to Gisbert, the problem is the fact that his conception of social reality is fundamentally inconsistent and hesitant, and is tied up with the way that the difference between the individual and society is inconsistently conceptualised. Modern psychology has removed the basis for the distinction between the two levels he suggests, but the argument for the existence of the social as an emergent synthesis was flawed in the beginning. In reality it is real individual men and women who are the component elements of society, not abstractions, and the object of sociology is the human fact in all its aspects: of the tendency to create super-human beings: 'Our generation knows only too well the kind of excess to which these give rise when applied to political or social practice' (1959: 367).

In the 1970s, when there developed a renewed interest in Durkheim's methodological writings, it emerged against the background of tenacious opinions (as identified by Nisbet). For example, in a generally interesting and accurate discussion of Durkheim's theory of morality, Wallwork stressed that the methodology actually practiced was quite different from the 'abstruse, positivistic statements of the *Rules*' (Wallwork, 1972: 6–7); the discussion of the normal and the pathological was 'probably the least successful piece of writing in all of Durkheim's work' (1972: 15). LaCapra dismissed the *Rules* as a simplistic imitation of Descartes (1972: 6). And in Britain Anthony Giddens concluded that,

Notwithstanding the fame which it has achieved, I think it is possible to claim that *The Rules of Sociological Method* is the weakest of Durkheim's major works: the principles set out therein were mainly received ideas, stated in a new form perhaps, but gaining most of their force from the polemical ardour with which they were advocated and the attractive simplicity of their presentation. (Giddens, 1977: 292)

Steven Lukes also reiterated the view that the *Rules* was a 'transitional point in (his) intellectual development'. The real break in his development occurred in 1898 with the 'analytical separation of socially given ideas, concepts, values and beliefs – or "collective *representations*" – as a crucial and relatively independent set of explanatory variables' (Lukes, 1973: 229).

More recent considerations do, however, seem to mark a new stage in the discussion. The first is by Jeffery Alexander in his *Theoretical Logic in Sociology*, which argues not that the *Rules* is merely a transitional work, but that it must be considered to be the work which 'marked a revolutionary break in [Durkheim's] theoretical thinking' (Alexander, 1982: 464). Whereas Lukes finds the first chapter of the *Rules* full of theoretical ambiguities and inconsistencies, Alexander claims that its simplicity is entirely apparent, not real, for it is the 'crucial break' (1982: 218). What had happened? Alexander points to a dramatic shift in the 'theory of structure'. Whereas in *The Division of Labour* interaction was conceived as 'instrumental', now in the *Rules* it is conceived as 'emotional': now 'social structure is a continuum stretching between rigidified and liquid emotions ... each ... structure has the same ontological status. Each is subjectively formed ...' (1982: 218–9). Consequently, then, the epistemology has become 'equally subjective' because 'actors know order not through its material constraint but through their subjective connection with its emotional essence' (1982: 219). The first chapter is revolutionary because it inverts Durkheim's conception of morphology, something which is acknowledged by Durkheim in his comment that previously he had made the mistake of 'presenting material density too much as the exact expression of dynamic density'. The *Rules* are not simply a retrospective endpiece to an early phase, they are 'prospective', since Durkheim's next major work 'closely follows the theoretical prolegomena that Durkheim laid out in 1894' (1982: 225).

The second more recent consideration, a long essay by Stephen Turner, begins with the surprising observation that 'Despite the voluminous Durkheim literature, there exists no adequate analysis of Durkheim's own philosophical account of the logic of explanations' (Turner, 1983-4: i, 425). This essay, far more modest than Alexander's, does not set out to establish a definitive answer to the problems of causality in Durkheim's theory. It simply begins to argue that Durkheim's arguments seem to be more complex than conventional accounts admit. It counters black or white interpretations with an attempt to disentangle Durkheim's own positions in the face of apparent inconsistencies. Looking at the concept of function, for example, he notes that 'Durkheim does not appeal to a "need for maintenance" or to a concept of equilibrium, or to a concept of functional necessity as the "functionalist" sociologies have done; far from 'smuggling teleology back in with the concept of function' in fact he banishes it 'more effectively' than previously. The outcome of the investigation is the conclusion that a verdict on the *Rules* must be based on a recognition that it is a propaedeutic, not a rationalisation of accomplished analyses.

The third, finally, is a radical essay by Warren Schmaus, concerned to refute the claim that Durkheim's position in the *Rules* is a simplistic empiricism. Again, like Turner, he picks up several important points of translation inaccuracy which have furnished the basis for misinterpretation and argues that perhaps the most important statement on methodology in the *Rules* is the following observation on the mistakes of the economists:

If 'value' had been studied by it ... as a reality ought to be, one would see the economist first indicate by what means one may recognise the thing called by this name, then classify its species, try to find by methodical inductions the causes as a function of which they vary, and finally compare these diverse results in order to extricate a general formula. (Schmaus, 1985: 13)

Schmaus then tries to show that these four basic steps are the main stages of Durkheim's own method, which is thus not empiricist at all but a consistent hypothetico-deductivist realist (1985: 2). Not only is there a complete internal consistency and continuity in Durkheim's work but the conception of method is in all respects identical with that of Comte.

11

Durkheim's Brief Reply to his Critics

This survey of the way the *Rules* has been read by sociologists reveals an astonishing diversity.

On the one hand are the views which claim that the work is naively scientistic, crudely and unreflectively empiricist, a radical or max-imallist positivism; on the other it has been called both a subjective and objective idealism, voluntaristic, even spiritualist. Others have suggested that the work oscillates between empiricism and idealism, nominalism and apriorism, and between subjectivism and objectivism. Another current of opinion suggests the work has to be situated in Durkheim's development from objectivism to subjectism, positivism to voluntarism; others have contested this evolutionism, stressing the remarkable continuities of themes and methods not only in Durkheim's work but in French social theory itself. Others have seen the work as fundamentally ambiguous, or as a fragile dialectical artifice, unable to stand up as consistent in any real test. Some have seen it as a genuine attempt to avoid the pitfalls of philosophical metaphysics and empiri-cal fragmentation, while others have rejected this, arguing that its solution is arbitrary or impossible. The philosophical basis of the work has been seen variously as Cartesian, Kantian, Hegelian, Comtean, Marxist, even compatible with Jamesean pragmatism. The political orientation has also been seen as a liberal socialism or proto-fascism. Some have argued that Durkheim had a specific propensity to think in contradictory terms.

Actually, Durkheim himself posed this very question about his work as a whole and asked rhetorically: 'Is this enterprise possible? Is it not

... contradictory in its terms?' (Durkheim, 1953: 70). The full argument is worth examining: the position

> without making itself systematically eclectic ... finds room for points of view which normally appear completely opposed. I wish to stress the fact that this science permits the empirical study of moral facts, while at the same time not destroying the *sui generis* religious character which is inherent in them and which distinguishes them from all other human phenomena. Thus we escape from utilitarian empiricism which, while claiming to offer a rational explanation of morality, denies its specific characteristics and reduces its fundamental ideas to those of economic techniques, as also from Kantian *a priorism*, which gives a fairly faithful analysis of the nature of morality but which describes more than it explains. We recognise the notion of duty, but for experimental reasons and without rejecting the valuable aspect of eudemonism. The fact of the matter is this: the different points of view which among moralists are in opposition are mutually exclusive only in the abstract. In fact they only express different aspects of a complex reality, and consequently all will be found in their various places when one brings one's mind to bear on this reality which one wishes to understand in its complexity. (1953: 62)

The difference between Durkheim and his readers, at least at the level of opinions on what the project involves, is clear. The critics accuse the method as either falling into a fixed naive position (either of empiricism or apriorism), or oscillating between empiricism and apriorism, or of being ambiguous in relation to them. Durkheim, on the other hand, claims to avoid the pitfalls of eclecticism, empiricism and apriorism, without any reduction to a single principle or the production of a naive synthesis through a purely logical dialectic. The problem, at this stage is: who is right?

Perhaps the question can be answered with reference to the *Rules*, and this seems to present a case *par excellence* of a remarkable divergence between the structures of its writing (as defined by Durkheim) and ways in which it has been read.

PART THREE

French sociology does not consider itself as an isolated discipline, working in its own specific field, but rather as a method....

(C. Lévi-Strauss)

12

Complex Transitions

Before attempting to provide a critical analysis of the arguments in the *Rules* it is necessary here to look at the nature of Durkheim's strategies, the way in which specific investigations were developed in a long term 'programme of research'. This has been the subject of a confused debate among Durkheim scholars. After examining the main issues of this debate, the problems of analysing Durkheim's strategic techniques will be discussed through investigations of the supple structure of his social theory, and his conception of pathways in complex transitions.

(i)

The contention that there are significant, even dramatic, shifts in Durkheim's thought is nothing new. Even in Durkheim's own lifetime there were writers who began to identify them (e.g. Davy, 1911: see discussion in Pickering, 1984: 48–50). Durkheim himself, of course, admitted that his ideas developed; in 1907 he reflected that it was in 1895 that he had really begun to understand how to study the importance of religion in social life and that all his 'previous research had to be started all over again so as to be harmonised with these new views' (Durkheim, 1982: 259). But what is the nature of such a process of 'harmonisation'?

Again other writers have noted an apparent epistemological switch in the shift from the evolutionary study of the *Division* to the synchronic study of *Suicide*. Yet others have argued that the later works not only concentrate more on the analysis of collective representations but involve a significant move away from positivistic to voluntaristic epistemological positions. More recently, as I have indicated, some current analyses have pushed this point of transition back to the first chapter of the *Rules* itself, while on the other hand there is a strong and growing body of thought which resists these conclusions, and suggests that it is the consistency and coherence of Durkheim's overall project which is the remarkable feature of his work.

Why this confusion? Can it be accounted for in relation to the texts? It seems clear from the exposition and analysis of the theoretical context of the *Rules* (in the previous part of this work) that Durkheim had a well-formulated general framework for sociology established by 1885–8 and this, with one or two significant modifications, remained constant throughout the thirty years of his subsequent career. Far from being an eclectic or inconsistent writer, what is remarkable is the degree of continuity and level of consistency Durkheim maintained in relation to this general framework. His conception of this framework is itself worth a comment. It is, he said in 1888, not a simple totality but a complex one divided into parts (Durkheim, 1978: 62); and this internal division was to be rethought as work progressed. This latter practice meant that the categories of sociology were to be modified as sociology itself developed. Durkheim's reflections on sociological method at the various stages of his career always included a consideration of its main branches. Mauss continued this practice after Durkheim's death, radically altering Durkheim's previous efforts (Mauss, 1968–9: iii, 178–245).

The internal division of intellectual labour, and its reordering, however, does rest on the premiss that *there is something to order*. Durkheim's project was from the beginning envisaged as contributing to the development of wide-ranging, mutually supporting specialist studies in a totalising sociology, and took up a position which had this as its ultimate aim. The brief essays of 1888 indicated a perspective in which this is given form: within the structure of the holistic thesis of the progressive evolution of societies through segmental to organised totalities many varied investigations could be located and existing work reorganised. If we take this as the central or core theoretical structure, even this might be thought to have been supplanted in Durkheim's development, for certainly the concept of 'mechanical' solidarity does not figure in the major study *Elementary Forms*, and the concept of 'anomic' phenomena does not figure after 1902 (Besnard, 1984: 46). One recent article has suggested the thematic framework of the organic division of labour also had been rejected by this later period as well (Pope and Johnson, 1983). This whole line of argument seems in danger, however, of introducing serious misunderstandings which arise because, once more, a fundamental idea is identified with one set of theoretical terms. If it is granted that the same problem, even the same idea, can be worked out in more than one set of theoretical formulations, the issue can be seen to concern the existence of possible alternative and progressive modes of investigating and exploring basic thematic issues. That Durkheim's essays and works continued in the framework of social evolution after 1902 cannot be doubted, nor that the later essays also dealt with problems of solidarity that had previously been thought out in terms of anomie.

It is necessary here to find means for making an important distinction: between the basic project of Durkheimian sociology and the specific theories which were developed at various stages of the overall programme. It is possible to clear up a number of misunderstandings if this is accomplished. It becomes necessary to distinguish between the development or modification within a theory, and large scale shifts between theories relative to the ideas of the basic project; it is also necessary to investigate the structure of the basic programme and the overall 'harmony' of the research strategies, but separately from the epistemological relations found in specific explorations. It might well be that there is a certain discontinuity between the specific theories while an underlying continuity exists in the basic project. On the other hand, however, the latter may also have been transformed, but almost certainly by another kind of process altogether; and this should not be assumed to have happened because a single or even a group of concepts have been dropped from the vocabulary for a certain period of time.

In order to forestall errors which arise from the reduction of theory to epistemology (e.g. by suggesting a new theory of religion inevitably involves an epistemological break), or the reduction of theoretical vocabulary to theory (e.g. the notion that an elaboration of a new terminology inevitably means the complete rejection of previous theory, etc.) it is necessary to establish first the real range of theories employed, and the range of terminologies employed, in the context of the basic principles of analysis and explanation adopted and promoted. If we take these precautions in relation to the *Rules* it becomes clear that it is a conditional statement among many others made on methodology, and can be assessed in relation to more fundamental objectives which hold together the various projects undertaken over a thirty year period. It is an error, for instance, to suggest that the work *Suicide* marks a break of any kind whether epistemological or theoretical simply because its analysis is 'synchronic' rather than 'diachronic'; it is, rather, a direct continuation and development of earlier 'synchronic' work devoted to the statistical examination of suicide and birth rates. It is also an error to suggest that because Durkheim became critical of analyses which assumed a one-to-one relationship between morphology and collective representations he was no longer interested in the role of morphology after 1898, etc. All of these misconceptions are the result of a failure to connect a particular alteration to, or modification of the wider programme and to examine the possible variations of method which can be adopted within the limits of such a programme.

The key to the investigation of Durkheim's development lies in the correct identification of the nature of the object of his sociology: the conception of society itself, the nature of its formation and transformation, and the relations of internal causality that are postulated as acting on its elements. In Durkheim's case the specifications of these elements are not given in a straightforward way, for he worked on a number of different levels of generality. But an approach to the question can be made via Durkheim's own indications of the way in which social species should be defined, how the relation between social facts should be conceived, and how societies were understood to be produced and reproduced.

Durkheim rejected the view that societies should be classified according to their level of civilisation or political form, or even economic or technological sophistication, but rather through the 'permanent substratum ... which alone can furnish the basis for a rational classification' (Durkheim, 1978: 263, cf., 1982: 117–18, n 10). This insistence seems to be a permanent feature of Durkheim's position, for it is clearly the basis of *Elementary Forms* in which Durkheim frequently cites the *Division*, even on points many assume to have been superseded, e.g. on the forces of the collective consciousness (see 1961: 238); on the externality of moral forces (1961: 264); as well as the significance of segmental morphology (1961: 115, cf., 225). Even the essay, claimed by some to be close to a Weberian analysis based on *verstehen* methods, 'Germany Above All' very explicitly acknowledges that it did not tackle the decisive analysis of the causes behind the outbreak of the war (Durkheim, 1915: 46).

The problem of morphology is raised in another form in the short entries in the *Année* 1899 and 1902 on morphology and civilisation (Durkheim, 1982: 241–4) which connect the two terms in a way that can serve as a basis for reading the comment on civilisation written in 1917 – though civilisations 'have a common basis, they resemble one another only in their most general characteristics' (Durkheim, 1978: 196). This point is important since there are many curious observations which might be thought simple waywardness if their conceptual basis is not understood. For example, in the *Division* Durkheim said:

> It may very well happen that in a particular society a certain division of labour, and notably the division of economic labour, may be greatly developed, although the segmental type may be strongly pronounced there. This seems to be the case with England. (1964a: 282)

And in the *Rules*, in a note added in 1901: 'Japan may borrow from us our arts, our industry and even our political organisation, but it will not cease to belong to a different social species from that of France and Germany' (1982: 118).

The methodological primacy of morphological as opposed to other social characteristics is a genuinely stable feature of the programme; in relation to this idea, however, there are many ways in which secondary characteristics may be grouped and analysed: for example, by its degree of civilisation, kinds of social conditions which exist historically, etc., but these are not decisive. It may also be possible to identify complications such as the idea that in 'exceptional' cases a division of labour may be developed in a rudimentary way but that the form of solidarity remain mechanical (an idea developed in the *Division*); on the other hand it is possible to examine the primary forms or social species without using the concept of morphology, even of segments, since Durkheim eventually began to deal with clans, tribes, and in relation to these 'matrimonial classes', etc. Durkheim seems to have remained faithful to the rule (derived from Spencer) that societies should be classified according to their degree of organisation or 'composition' (into species) and to the extent that their parts had fused or coalesced (into varieties). All other characteristics, he maintained, were less stable, or less fundamental.

But there is an important theoretical development indicated by Durkheim himself which occurred around 1894, concerning his sociology of religion. The full impact of this change can be seen by comparing the *Division* with his essay on incest of 1897 (see Gane,

1983b). In place of a theory of the secular increase in volume of society in which a prime role in methodology is acceded to morphology in the explanation of the process of the formation of societies, the new emphasis on the power of the sacred meant that societies were born divided into sexual groups, in processes approximating to cultural revolutions. A great many elements of the social theory were thus perforce reorganised: for example, instead of describing primitive societies as lacking general concepts, of living at the level of sensations (determined by morphological constraints) (Durkheim, 1964b: 290), all societies were to be seen as dominated by forces acting at the level of social ideals (including the conceptual hierarchy (also note, constrained by morphology)).

It seems true to say that the role and action of morphological factors were given greater scope in the earlier period, but two comments should be made. The first is that those interpretations which have tried to insist on the idea that Durkheim changed focus from morphological facts towards collective representations ignore the fact that the object of the *Division* was law and social sanction, i.e., moral phenomena; and secondly that Durkheim refused to find another way, other than via morphology, of classifying social types. Instead of holding, however, to the view (with the exception noted) that material or physical densities are exact expressions of moral or dynamic densities (1964b: 282; 1982: 146), after 1894 his conception of the relation of social parts developed away from such tight 'expressive' causality. In 1898 he wrote that social facts could be thought of as being of two orders, both produced 'in' and 'by' society, (i.e. there were secondary social facts which produced a whole world of phenomena independently of social morphology or even the primary facts of social consciousness to which they could not be reduced (indeed, it is this thought which is developed in the comments in the Introduction to *Elementary Forms* where the choice of the simplest religious forms (thought by Durkheim to be Australian totemism) is justified in terms of the absence of secondary complicating structures)).

Such a dramatic development seems to be paralleled in Durkheim's addition of a further avenue for identifying social facts: those which act on the individual not from without but from within:

> Society commands us because it is exterior and superior to us ... on the other hand it is within us and *is* us, we ... desire it, albeit with a *sui generis* desire since, whatever we do, society ... dominates us infinitely. ((1906) Durkheim, 1953: 57)

and by the further division of the *collective conscience* into moral and intellectual facts (1953: 95–6). These new categories, it was argued, simply completed the view that fact and value were inseparable and that moral constraint was no 'more than the material and apparent expression of an interior and profound fact which is whole ideal: this is *moral authority*' (Durkheim, 1961: 239). This suggests that the conception of the social frame, as a whole, was conceived as a social soul: an ideality contained within a body conceived as a material, physical condensation or crystallisation acting as a 'support', but not as simple epiphenomenon of it (Durkheim, 1970: 314–15).

Durkheim believed, even in the early period, that material density was the expression of the active forces of moral density, but that material densities 'indirectly' constrained the movements of moral agents. In his critique of Saint-Simon (1896) he roundly criticised theories which sought 'the moral rule from economic matter'. It must be put the other way, he said: 'to discover through science the moral restraint which can regulate economic life' (Durkheim, 1960a: 285). But it would be wrong to deduce that, for Durkheim, physical constraints were the only ones, for the register of consolidated social phenomena far exceeded simple materialisation: it included a whole order of crystallised moral institutions, which, though acting in their own right, also acted as constraints on social currents.

Though brief, this review of the main developments in Durkheim's sociology suggests there were important anchoring points in a programme which evolved increasingly complex conceptions of the social whole, its modalities of change, and increasingly sophisticated styles of sociological explanation.

(ii)

But what is the nature of the strategic component of this programmatic sociology? The idea that sociology must follow a special, sinuous, even 'devious' (1970: 311) path in order for it to reach its objectives was clearly one of Durkheim's main justifications to a recourse to methodological reflection. The contention here is that readings which ignore or fail to understand the nature of this path and its relation to the underlying rationale of the strategic elements of the project as a whole (as realised in Durkheim's various works, and as described in the *Rules*) miss what is essential in the whole sociological enterprise itself. Integral to the practice of the new sociology was the attempt to escape traditional boxes: it was not empiricist or apriorist, not materialist or idealist, not nominalist or realist, etc.:

> the rationalism which is immanent in the sociological theory of knowledge is ... midway between classical empiricism and apriorism. (Durkheim, 1961: 31)

> If you defend sociology against materialist metaphysics, and that alone, you will be accused of wanting a metaphysical sociology of spiritualist tendency. Now the latter is no less of an obstacle than the former, in fact if not in principle. (Besnard, 1983: 29)

> the notion of social species has ... the very great merit advantage of providing us with a middle term (*un moyen term*) between ... the nominalism of the historians and the extreme realism of the philosophers. (Durkheim, 1982: 108 mod.)

When Durkheim was accused of being an empiricist or a realist he rejected the charge as a failure to understand and grasp the orientation of the project. This was precisely to avoid either entrapment in these camps or an eclectic combination of them. The way that sociology could avoid these pitfalls was to find, progressively, tactical pathways between these oppositions, to live in the tensions between them, by elaborating multiphased and multifacetted epistemological strategies. This idea had the advantage, he said, of opening up ways of approaching new problems, new routes by finding the links in the chain of progressive research. He could not accept that it was to work on purely ideational phenomena (sciences do not have ideas as their raw material), but neither could it work purely on sensations by means of sensations. Sociology metaphorically borrows the concepts of established sciences as controls, and seeks a way of establishing an objective and reliable representation of objects conceived as being tied to a world lying outside of its conceptions. Whatever risk there was in being stigmatised as materialist or empiricist, Durkheim insisted on the radical element of the empirical as a fundamental moment in research. For example, in proposing to work in stages from the superficial external characteristics towards the internal realities, these 'external' features 'however superficial ... show to the scientist the path that he must follow ... they are the first and indispensable link in the chain' (Durkheim, 1982: 81). Indeed, a specific link between the observer and the observed could be established, since the preliminary matter of sociology existed within the world as already represented: and 'what realism is there in saying that *inside the facts* (and not outside them) there exists a category with specific characteristics, which consequently must be abstracted ... and studied separately?' (Besnard, 1983: 41).

Society naturally produces the raw materials by which social science may advance (i.e. phenomena with the characteristic of being 'consolidated' or existing in a collective form independently from individuals). These are to be valued in sociology not out of deference to some positivistic metaphysic, but as a necessary first contact with the object in the investigatory process. As such these materials neither contain in themselves some essence which is to be extracted by the investigator, as the truth of the fact, nor are they self-revealing. The appropriate method to be applied to the analysis of these facts is, therefore, one which involves artifice, both comparative (either generic or genetic) and logical. All that is required by way of methodological assumption is a belief in the necessary and intrinsic connection of the superficial external characteristics with the deeper realities, and the legitimacy of the attempt to apply the scientific principle of causality to human affairs.

If Durkheim's project is examined in this light, its epistemological rules are thought subordinate to the stages through which it must pass. During the first stages the initial definitions and their modifications are in close proximity to common definitions, and saturated with empiricist elements; but as work in the scientific discipline advances so does the distance from these elements increase – in the first instance by the processes of rational criticism and by the introduction of more and more reliable instruments for the production of information. At later stages, there is a progressive break even with the external comparative work on the surface of things. This break does not at all abolish the empirical moment, it simply enables what has been previously known as empirical to be recast in a more adequate frame of knowledge. An eventual fusion of the external with the internal (Durkheim, 1982: 70) is anticipated. It is not useful, according to Durkheim, to think of this process as moving from an empiricism to a realism. The strategy is to pass consistently and continuously in *between* nominalism and realism. If it is to be called a position of scientific rationalism, a rationalism appropriate to sociology, i.e., a complex rationalism, able to resist theoretical reductionism.

Durkheim's claim to find a position 'midway' between the two poles, or to find a 'middle term' which is not reducible to the other two, must be considered in relation to the course of the overall project itself. This may be one way of examining the problem of the nature of contradiction, for just as Durkheim claims that social reality is complex, and that apparent contradiction is an effect of a certain type of illegitimate theoretical homogenisation or levelling (Durkheim, 1953: 62), so the complexity of the sociological project involves a recognition of the true dispersal of different positions between the stages envisaged; and that apparent contradictions arise because the stages are conflated (a different form of levelling). There are other complexities which have to be acknowledged: for example, the elaboration of alternative sets of method and alternative tactics available within the overall trajectory of the project. A particular tactic may not be the ideal one but forced on the researcher by necessities (Durkheim, 1978: 210; 1970: 146). And almost all the possible tactics have certain disadvantages, or costs (choosing the most consolidated facts ignores the currents which may be more profound phenomena; choosing the currents may lose in objectivity, etc.). The complexity here reflects orders of priority in research.

What figures in thought as a direct contradiction, Durkheim suggests then, is the product of putting mutually exclusive terms together on the same plane, or in the same 'moment' of argument; and, in this perspective, it might be possible to look at one of the most blatant of 'contradictions': the very examination of social phenomena as things. Durkheim himself realised this: 'the thing', he said 'stands in opposition to the idea' (Durkheim, 1982: 35), and, as his conception of sociology was 'in part an application of the (spiritualist) principle to social facts' (1982: 32, note that this was also implied in the *Division* (Durkheim, 1964b: 348)), even a 'hyper-spiritualism' (1953: 34), there was an apparent paradox at the heart of the project itself. Yet the idea that this is a real paradox, or a metaphysics, is discussed and rejected on both points: the recommendation of treating social facts as things is not to say that they are material things; and to say that the property of the social is a specific spirituality does not mean that it cannot be studied as a natural phenomenon:

> despite its metaphysical appearance, this word designates nothing more than a body of natural facts which are explained by natural causes. It does, however, warn us that the new world thus opened to science surpasses all in complexity. (Durkheim, 1953: 34)

In order to avoid the dangers of reductions implied in materialism and idealism, the term 'hyperspiritualism' was proposed as the general definition of the nature of the object of sociology. Again, this would, he said, be parallel to what has happened in psychology: a

> *spirituality* by which we characterise intellectual facts ... has become itself the object of positive science, and that, between the ideology of the introspectionists and biological naturalism, a psychological naturalism has been founded ... A similar transformation should take place in sociology. (1953: 32)

This does not resolve the problem. There is a reappearance of the dilemma in two forms: one concerns the charge that here Durkheim has violently inserted an unnecessary a priori preconception as to the nature of social facts, and the other concerns the idealist implications for the consequent analysis of causal relationships in sociological analysis. For the moment, however, it is possible from previous analysis to say that Durkheim's position held that, although the conception of the moral fact was certainly developed in terms of *spirituality*, this was conceived as a term designed to avoid the problems of idealist metaphysics, while the formulation of social causation determined by such a range of 'natural facts' could work directly as moral or ideal facts, i.e., 'stem' from them *via* facts of the physical order (morphology). In this way the traditional opposition between the mind and the body is posed in a new form: the mind is not, he said, some mystic substance located either in or outside the body, conceived as purely physical or as reducible to the latter alone (idealistic monism and empirical monism, Durkheim, 1960b: 330). Looking at the 'dualism' of human nature, and rejecting Pascal's idea that man is a 'monster of contradictions', Durkheim's solution was to differentiate individual from social phenomena, and then to see in the former a closer link with the physical body: then the complexity is not contradictory for

> the things that embody the collective representations arouse the same feelings as do the mental states that they represent and, in a manner of speaking, materialise ... Consequently they are not placed on the same plane as ... things that interest only our physical individualities ... Therefore, we assign them a completely different place in the complex of reality ... This system of conceptions is not purely imaginary. (Durkheim, 1960a: 336)

By adopting such an approach, sociology is able to avoid analyses which 'eliminate the problem' in their very solution, and to provide an explanation of how the apparent contradiction arises. The result is the thesis that the elements exist in a heterogeneous complex whole but without logical contradiction.

(iii)

The particularity of Durkheim's vision seems to be evident at two sites: the notion of the complexity of social reality as a totality, and the theory of progressive complexity of transformations. It is possible to find a link between the two themes in the sense that the idea of an adequate practice is itself founded on the criticism of the disastrous practical results of both mystical conservatism and ultra-revolutionism. In the various considerations of moral education, Durkheim explicitly developed this theme:

> it seemed that to secularise education, all that was needed was to take out of it every supernatural element. A simple stripping operation was supposed to have the effect of disengaging rational morality from adventitious and parasitical elements that cloaked it and prevented it from realising itself.... In reality the task was much more complex. It was not enough to proceed by simple elimination to reach the proposed goal. On the contrary, a profound transformation was necessary. (1973b: 8)

Social complexity implies the interconnectedness of things which have taken time to form and to combine together. Thus there are disastrous consequences for a practice of dealing with it which does not realise this nature. The emergence of a secular morality had been underway for centuries, indeed 'if ever a revolution has been long in the making, this is it' (1973b: 7). The difficulty, he suggested, lay in the fact that religious symbols were not simply laid on top of a rational moral system when they might be lifted off, 'finding in a state of purity and isolation a self-sufficient rational morality'. Rather:

> these two systems of beliefs and practices have been too inextricably bound together in history ... some elements of both systems approached each other to the point of merging and forming only one system.... Consequently, if ... one confines himself to withdraw from moral discipline everything that is religious without replacing it, one almost inevitably runs the danger of withdrawing at the same time all elements that are properly moral ... it is imperative not to be satisfied with a superficial separation. (1973b: 8–9)

By implication, a 'simple' revolution might be conceived in circumstances where a parasitic superstructure could be removed; or, alternatively, where an already existing pure system could be imposed (say, for example, an already perfectly formed enlightenment on ignorance). Durkheim's main point was that complex struggle is the rule, and that only on condition 'we do not delude ourselves concerning these difficulties will it be possible to triumph over them' (1973b: 7).

If we return to the *Rules*, there is no doubt that the process of scientific development in sociology is, too, regarded as a complex transformation process (Durkheim, 1982: 71). But in dealing with the relation of sociology to political parties and doctrines, Durkheim's position was to advocate the independence of sociology from all such interest groups: it will be, he said,

> neither individualist, communist or socialist, in the sense commonly attributed to those words ... this is not to say that sociology should profess no interest in practical questions. On the contrary, it has been seen that our constant preoccupation has been to guide it towards some practical outcome.... But the role of sociology, from this viewpoint, must consist precisely in liberating us from all parties. This will be done not so much by opposing one doctrine to other doctrines, but by causing those minds confronted with these questions to develop a special attitude ... it alone can teach us to treat, with respect but without idolatry, historical institutions of whatever kind, by causing us to be aware, at one and the same time, of what is necessary and provisional about them, their strength of resistance and their infinite variability. (1982: 161)

It is important to remember (with its caveat) that Durkheim also wrote: 'our method is by no means revolutionary. In one sense it is even essentially conservative, since it treats social facts as things whose nature, however flexible and malleable it may be, is still not modifiable at will....' (1982: 32).

The parallels between the theoretical and the practical are consistent, and many examples could be given. Just one more will suffice – the concept of discipline itself. This has many aspects, as I have mentioned in an earlier chapter: it is central to Durkheim's concept of socialism as a social form (see particularly Durkheim, 1964b: 409); to the concept of education (see the lectures on discipline, 1973b: 17–63); and to the concept of science. They have something in common, of course, for 'methodological rules are for science what rules of law and custom are for conduct' (Durkheim, 1964b: 367). If discipline has an effect *sui generis* in every society, the systems of discipline are transformed in different circumstances. If they fall below a certain limit, severe anomic crises can result. The way that these limits were conceived is illustrated in the following discussion of moral education, but the discussion could be extended to intellectual education as will be shown:

> Of course, we do set ourselves a line of conduct, and we say, then, that we have set up rules of conduct of such and such a sort. But the word so used generally lacks its full meaning. A plan of action that we ourselves outline, which depends only upon ourselves and that we can always modify is a

project, not a rule. Or, if it is to some extent truly independent of our will, it must rest in the same degree on something other than our will. . . . For example, we adopt a given mode of life because it carries the authority of science; the authority of science legitimates it. It is to the science that we defer, in our behaviour, and not to ourselves. (1973: 28–9)

The discipline so conceived must be able to establish both attainable goals and point to effective means: it is a moral/intellectual project. The effect of discipline

by no means implies, however, that man must arrive at some fixed position where ultimately he finds tranquility. In intermittent steps one can pass from one special task to others equally specific, without drowning in the dissolving sense of limitlessness. The important thing is that behaviour have a clear-cut objective, which may be grasped and which limits and determines it. (1973: 40)

(iv)

We are now in a position to grasp the coherence of the strategic dynamic of Durkheim's project as a whole and to see the role of the *Rules* within it. It can be recalled that Tarde's accusation – that Durkheim's concept of constraint figured as a constituent concept in the sociology – was rejected by Durkheim on the grounds that Tarde had mistaken a sign for the thing itself. But the concept of discipline seems to be more than a sign. In an important section in the *Rules* (Ch. 5, iv), Durkheim contrasted different theories of spontaneity and constraint, and suggested that constraint is natural and spontaneous. The discussion, however, moved from that of constraint as a 'characteristic' of the social fact, to the more fundamental issue of 'social discipline':

to most of the attempts that have been made to explain social facts rationally, the possible objection was either that they did away with any idea of social discipline, or that they only succeeded in maintaining it with the assistance of deceptive subterfuges. The rules we have set out would, on the other hand, allow a sociology to be constructed which would see in the spirit of discipline the essential condition for all common life. (Durkheim, 1982: 144)

The idea of social discipline seems to indicate something about the social fact which is more than superficial, and this view is confirmed in the lectures on *Moral Education*, where, having discussed the important structures of regularity and authority in morality, he argued at the root of the moral life there is, besides a preference for regularity, the notion of moral authority. Furthermore, these two aspects of morality are closely linked, their unity deriving from a more complex idea that embraces both of them ... the concept of discipline. (1973b: 31)

If moral discipline realises its authority in acts which are purely moral (i.e., they transcend utilitarian considerations), it is true that intellectual discipline realises its authority in its search for scientific truth (which also transcends utilitarian functions). Science is characterised by this discipline and its specific consequences, not by the rule of anarchic intellectual individualism. It is not a game, whimsical puzzle-solving, but, *par excellence*, the new serious life with its own devotions.

Here, then, we reach the central issue: if it is acceptable for sociologists to study 'primitive religions' sociologically, i.e. to treat these religions as having social causes at work in them, the idea that modern science also has social causes in them conflicts with the widely held view that science transcends its social determinations. Durkheim noted the problem here in a review of 1910:

the pursuit of science is an eminently social matter, however great a role individuals may fill. It is social because it is the product of a vast cooperative effort ... because it presupposes certain methods and techniques that are the creation of an authoritative tradition ... because it brings into play ideas that dominate all thought and seemingly condense – classify by categories – the whole civilisation.... (Durkheim, 1980: 109).

Durkheim's idea of the nature of science, and particularly of scientific truth, is worth noting at this point in detail, as he said in his lectures on pragmatism and sociology: it involves the conceptualisation of science as a social institution with a specific type of development and ideal:

it came into existence in Greece, and nowhere else, to meet certain needs. For both Plato and Socrates, the role of science is to unify individual judgments. The proof is that the method used to construct it is 'dialectics', or the art of comparing contradictory human judgments with a view to finding those in which there is agreement. If dialectics is the first among scientific methods, and its claim is to eliminate contradictions, it is because the role of science is to turn minds towards impersonal truths and to eliminate contradictions and particularisms. (Durkheim, 1983: 88)

The new kind of reason which science develops is linked to a recognition of the complexity (heterogeneity, variability, multiplicity) of things, is connected to the fact that 'the conditions of life in society are more complex' (1983: 72); a new relation between truth and individual diversity is also established, for, unlike earlier forms of thought where individuals were united into a single collective consciousness, here individuals 'communicate in one object which is the same for all, with each, however, retaining his own personality' (1983: 88). This diversity is also associated with the rise of scientific tolerance:

> Every object of knowledge offers an opportunity for an infinity of possible points of view, such as the point of view of life, of purely mechanical movement, of stasis and dynamics, of contingency and determination, of physics and biology and so on ... there are different but equally justified ways of examining it. These are probably partial truths, but all these partial truths come together in the collective consciousness and find their limits and their necessary complements.... Everyone must be able to admit that someone else has perceived an aspect of reality, which he himself had not grasped, but which is as real and as true as those to which he had gone from preference. (1983: 91–2)

This passage is highly significant, and may be taken as something of a reflection on Durkheim's whole sociological project, with its apparently inflexible insistence on the one scientific method. Here the unity of science is not found in the existence of one method, but that different methods come to play the role of mutual checking mechanisms in a diversity. The purely deterministic orientation, he says, is, in principle, only one possibility among many, all of which have equal claims to validity. Such a social project is not only infinitely diverse but recognises that the search for truth can never be finally attained, a theme evident in the *Rules*:

> we must approach the social domain from those positions where the foothold for scientific investigation is the greatest possible. Only later will it be feasible to carry our research further and by progressive approaches gradually capture that fleeting reality which the human mind will perhaps never grasp completely. (Durkheim, 1982: 83)

New problems enter the picture here as it becomes apparent that science is the heir of the religious inheritance. Do we move from the dominance of the sacred/profane opposition to that of truth/error opposition? Unlike Saint Simon and Comte, who thought a new form of Christianity might be evolved, Durkheim is consistent in his view that it is the state which organises the social cult (Durkheim, 1957: 70), and it is the University which provides the institutional support for the social sciences. Scientific truths, he said in the lectures on pragmatism, have all the intrinsic characteristics of collective representations: it is science itself which possesses the authority of the social fact. The problem remains: how do sociological truths become dominant collective representations? Two answers seem to have been provided. One through (reproductive) institutions like the school system; the other through large scale collective (creative and recreative) effervescences.

(v)

In order to complete the circle of analysis here it would be necessary to find in Durkheim's work a consideration of dialectical and scientific reason as social phenomena, situated relative to morphological and representational structures. This work does not exist; but it is possible to discuss Durkheim's ideas as they appear in *Educational Thought*, the text which comes closest to meeting these requirements, and indeed some of Durkheim's commentators have noticed this without taking up the idea (Wallwork, 1972: 130–46; Lukes, 1973: 383; Fenton, 1984: 152–61). I have already pointed out the aims of this work in an early chapter; here I shall note that the crucial turning points in the development of education in France were the crisis at the beginning of the sixteenth century (the Renaissance) (Durkheim, 1977: 225), and that of the mid-eighteenth century (the Enlightenment) (1977: 293). Durkheim's analysis, in brief, was that Renaissance Humanism rapidly dismantled education based on the scholastic dialectic (1500–30) but only to produce an educational doctrine promoting an aesthetic and less-than-serious emphasis on rhetoric. The reaction to this crisis enabled the Jesuits to establish a firm hold within French education, and its ironic consequence was to negate successfully the subtleties of the Humanists and to move towards dogmatism, simplism but also clarity (and this was the base from which the tradition known as Cartesianism grew). The movements which developed against this in the eighteenth century, deriving in part from German protestantism, inaugurated a new phase of rationalism by pointing to the necessity of an educational doctrine which embraced the teaching of the scientific knowledge of things outside of man conceived as essentially complex. But the social experiments of the Revolution, which tried to institute a new educational regime based on the ideas of the encyclopaedists, were lost in the early nineteenth century with the restoration, and things returned to the critical state they were in in the *ancien regime*. The new ideas, however,

> were to survive the backlash which, albeit falteringly, occupied the greater part of the nineteenth century and which proved so difficult to overcome.... The result is that the academic history of the nineteenth century was not very rich in innovations; it was a slow, gradual rediscovery of ideas which were already well known to the eighteenth century.... (1977: 305)

This general history allows us to find the theses behind many of Durkheim's repeated formulas about the unique conditions of French culture which permitted the emergence of sociology: the faith in reason and clarity derives from the Jesuits (1977: 275), the emergence of complex rationalism and the need to treat objects as things with Condorcet and Diderot (1977: 291–6), the need to restore elements lost in the Renaissance (dialectic) and the Revolution (complex rationalism). It also clarifies Durkheim's apprehensions about social reaction, for Renaissance progress was negated through Jesuit counter-reformation and the Revolution's gains were wiped away in the counterrevolution. But crucially, for the argument of this particular chapter, it is the clarification in this history of the specifically Durkheimian conceptions of the dialectic, scientific logic and modes of observation which is significant.

Two chapters concerning the teaching of the dialectic in the medieval Universities (Chs 12–13) can be profitably examined, for they deal with issues which far transcend those topics. The basic processes of Aristotelean dialectic are examined and compared directly with the experimental logic of scientific investigation which emerged in the Renaissance (outside of the Universities). Both are fundamentally forms of dialectic: one confronts opinions, the other facts (1977: 154). But their structures are very different. Aristotelean dialectic works towards plausible, probable truth; Aristotle

> imposes upon himself as a strict methodological rule to assemble and examine the different solutions which his predecessors had given to this problem, so that he could set them beside his own, so that he could examine them simultaneously, in other words so that he could debate with them. (1977: 146)

But, following the decisive reform of the theory of observation in the Renaissance, which aimed at 'producing a combination of observations, such that a conclusion can be derived in the same way that the conclusion of a syllogism is derived from its premisses' (1977: 150), conclusive experiments can be undertaken, parallel with those in geometry, which once accomplished are 'true for all time ... valid for all countries and all ages' (1977: 152). Durkheim cited the example of the progress in the theory of anthrax and its practical consequence in the development of vaccination. But as there are limits to the growth of such sciences, especially when applied to social phenomena, a form of dialectic will always be required:

we must proceed as best we can by means of analogies, comparisons, generalisations, suppositions, in a word by using dialectic. And since the conclusions which we reach by this kind of reasoning can at best be probable they nevertheless raise the possibility of controversy. (1977: 154)

The 'aggressive, total and contemptuous rejection of dialectic' in the Renaissance 'was not justified' (1977: 151); in fact no such elimination could ever be justified, since the scope of science is always restricted to a part of the totality: there must be recourse to dialectic, which means 'bringing (propositions) together and confronting them with one another ... that is why, with respect to questions of this sort, argument must necessarily always have the last word' (1977: 150).

Even in modern times, in the analysis of social phenomena above all, there are 'controversial areas' and will always be, however much experimental reason drives back the 'frontiers of the controversial' (1977: 155).

But in the end, Durkheim is sure that the future advance of the application of experimental reason to the social sphere is essential. So the detours describe a circle:

Although it is orientated towards the outside it leads us away from ourselves only to bring us back to ourselves; but it brings us back armed with, and enriched by, precious insights which cast new light upon our own nature. (1977: 342)

13

A Closer Look at the Emergence of the *Rules*

Apply yourself scrupulously to the study of a great master; dismantle a system down to its most secret workings.
(attributed to Durkheim)

Although the situation is now beginning to change, most sociologists still treat the *Rules* as a single, if flawed, statement of methodological dogma and assume that Durkheim conceived it as an expression of a projected final summation of methodological intent. They also think Durkheim simply abandoned this positional document as he began to move away, in the late 1890s, from the allegedly rather crude orientations embodied in the *Division* of 1893.

It is clear from the evidence I have presented in earlier chapters that this view must be abandoned. The *Rules* does not stand on its own, even in the years 1893–4 when it was composed. It certainly has a higher individual profile than other statements which might be taken as key statements of Durkheimian methodology, and this tendency (encouraged in part by Durkheim himself) has been continued by the policies of English publishers (for instance the new translation of the *Division* omits these important complementary passages); but if the *Rules* is placed in adequate perspective, it is evident not only that it develops ideas formulated in the years 1887–8, but also that the full 1893 Introduction to the *Division* is a dress rehearsal, at least of the first three chapters.

This is not the end of the story, however, for the book entitled *The Rules of Sociological Method* (of 1895) differs in important respects from the series of articles of the same name published in 1894. Its second edition (of 1901) also contains important additions and these should be seen against the methodological works of that period written by Durkheim, Mauss and Fauconnet.

It will be argued here that the *Rules* is part of a continuous reflection on method and research strategy and not as Durkheim's unsuccessful attempt to write a definitive methodological treatise. The main analysis here will concern the years between 1893–5 (placed against the larger background of the work between 1888–1901) and will attempt to distinguish between illusory and real development.

SOCIAL AND MORAL FACTS

From social to moral facts (1888–93)?

In Durkheim's initial formulations of the object of sociology, the dominant term established was clearly that of the *social fact* (Durkheim, 1978: 62). In enunciating the terrain of sociology, he suggested four main sub-divisions: 1. the general field of common beliefs (ideas and sentiments) which are passed from generation to generation; 2. the area of morality which is identified as that section of culture where maxims and rules are accompanied by specific social sanctions; 3. dividing this field itself is the important line between morality and law – the latter is more crystallised and has a specific institutional support (which may be sub-divided into types of law), and 4. economic phenomena. (He noted that this inventory was incomplete, but adequate as an outline (1978: 64).) In developing the approach to the study of the family, the sociologist must search, he argued, for both statistical and ethnographic evidence: the former makes possible the analysis of fluid social phenomena, the latter facilitates the analysis of phenomena 'already determined and consolidated' (1978: 217). In the early project on the sociology of the family, outlined in 1888, Durkheim argued that by looking at the customs and laws so defined, the sociologist would be in a position to distinguish between habitual individual practices and socially sanctioned conduct (constituent of the social structure of the societies analysed).

In the project realized in the *Division* this methodological perspective was continued with the modification that the main focus became that range of phenomena which had the specific characteristic of being socially sanctioned; Durkheim called this the terrain of 'moral facts' and continued to develop the distinction between moral facts sanctioned by public opinion and moral facts sanctioned by the state as law. His thesis attempted to show that types of law (and therefore types of sanction) reflected different social structures. This idea was complemented by an attempt to distinguish between normal and abnormal developments in these social structures. In the 'Introduction' (1893) to the work he outlined the principles of a definition of moral fact (as comprising sanctioned norms) and those for the distinction between normal and abnormal moral facts. Elsewhere the work elaborated the principles for the classification of social types, and the main forms of sociological as opposed to historical-teleological demonstration, i.e., the comparative method.

From moral to 'consolidated' social facts (1893–4)?

The 'Introduction' to the *Division* emphasised the great differences between moral and more general social facts in terms of the nature of the constraints involved. Moral sanctions are both socially organised and act 'with true necessity' which is 'predetermined even in its modalities' (Durkheim, 1964b: 424). But deviations from rules which are not sanctioned in this manner succeed or fail not only on the basis of contingent factors. Durkheim provided a number of examples of nonsanctioned procedures: the technical aspects of a doctor's course of medical treatment, the technical processes of the manufacturer, the merchant, the artist (1964b: 424); the free forms of pleasure in sport, aesthetic pursuits, gifts and sacrifices 'that no duty demands' (430). These are contingent acts which are not socially regulated. The contingent successes or failures of the former rest on chance factors coming into play, and individual free variation may give rise to rapid innovation; in the latter the contingency is related to the fact that the acts are superfluous, unnecessary, gratuitous. That these sanctions are both profoundly social and externally organised (i.e., not a simple form of social consciousness) made them ideal objects of sociological analysis. Non-sanctioned practices had the drawback of lacking both these features. Durkheim drew the distinction between these two types of practice so firmly that he even suggested that: 'it would be contrary to all method to unite under one rubric acts which are compelled to conform to a pre-established rule and others which are free from all regulation' (1964b: 429).

Durkheim indicated that what is important is the specific nature of social sanctions compared with other constraints on action: the form of the predetermination, uniquely, is known in advance. Whereas: 'the consequences which arise from ignoring principles of traditional technique are the most contingent' (1964b: 425).

In the *Rules* the tone changed: 'as an industrialist nothing prohibits me from working with procedures and methods of a previous century; but if I tried I would certainly ruin myself' (Durkheim, 1982: 51, trans mod).

Here the emphasis ceased to be the element of contingency, it became, virtually, its opposite – the certainty of the effect of constraint. Alteration reflects the fact that the objective of Durkheim's argument had altered: he now wished to define the social fact as a force which constrains the action of individuals. Here the social fact includes the moral fact as one of its forms of imposition through sanction.

Thus the argument had two sides: the kind of rule and the kind of constraint. In the (1893) Introduction Durkheim insisted on the role of the sanction as a force which imposed the way of acting on the individual. The individual does not go through long abstract theoretical arguments to reach a choice of action: moral forms 'are specific and definite ways of acting imposed upon us' (Durkheim, 1964b: 420). In 1894 Durkheim reached a definition of the social fact as 'any way of acting ... capable of exerting over the individual an external constraint' (Durkheim, 1982: 59), and argued this by distinguishing between 'the existence of some determinate sanction [and] the resistance that the fact opposes to any individual action' (1982: 56–7 mod). Thus moral duty via sanction was a direct imposition of a way of acting, whereas the force of circumstance (technology, etc.) constrained without making a moral demand as such.

Clearly the argument of 1894 reiterates that of 1888 in the sense that it outlined modalities of the social fact (the continuum of degrees of consolidation), together with modalities of social inquiry (from comparative method to objective indices and statistics). In the *Division* research focussed on types of law and sanction, and this preference was adhered to in the 1894 version of the *Rules* (not available in English), where it is insisted that the sociologist must analyse social facts which exhibit a 'sufficient degree of consolidation'.

From 'consolidated' to 'isolated' social facts (1894–5)?
In 1895 this was altered, in the book version, to a rule calling for the sociologist to give privileged place to social facts existing naturally isolated 'from their individual manifestations' (Durkheim, 1982: 83).

What had happened to impel Durkheim to make this alteration? It is very likely that Durkheim had decided between these two versions to undertake the project on suicide, an analysis of statistical representations of suicide currents (a project first announced in 1895 (Durkheim, 1978: 181)). These are clearly not social facts in consolidated forms, quite the reverse. But as Durkheim had signalled the legitimacy of studying these phenomena as social facts in the early period (1888), he was simply refocusing research priorities, and in no sense manufacturing an epistemological transformation, as so many commentators claim.

Towards exclusively ideal moral and intellectual causation (1895–1901)?

The 1901 edition of the *Rules* made a small number of important additions to the text and possessed an important new Preface which sought to discuss and refute criticisms which had been made of the first edition. In the second Preface he attempted to counter suggestions that the definition of the social fact (as exerting an external constraint) would include most natural, not social, phenomena by saying that there were two types of constraint and they were of quite different orders: 'What is exclusively peculiar to social constraint is that it stems not from the unyieldingness of certain patterns of molecules, but from the prestige with which certain representations are endowed' (Durkheim, 1982: 44).

Again, this formulation has led a number of commentators to suggest that Durkheim had now definitively left behind his 'crude' emphasis on material densities, etc., and had begun to construct a theory emphasising the nature and role of representations. Actually, Durkheim's formulation is a characteristic one: he does not say that physical causation plays no part in social causation, nor that representations are the exclusive terrain of sociology. Indeed, in the companion piece to the Preface, the article 'Sociology and its Scientific Field' (1900) emphasises the significance of the analysis of the physical substratum (Durkheim, 1960b: 360), as did his special note (1899) the *Année* on social morphology (Durkheim, 1982: 241–2).

Should the theme here be investigated further by looking at a sequence of statements beyond 1901, it would not be difficult to locate in 1906, for instance, another posing of the question 'by what characteristics can we recognise and distinguish moral facts?' His answer, that they can be recognised through the action of both negative *and* positive sanctions, adds a further element: 'desirability is the second characteristic of all moral facts' (Durkheim, 1953: 41–5). This development has led some commentators, by failing to establish the nature of Durkheim's project, to see yet another revolution in his intellectual biography.

It is very easy now to see how Durkheim's texts have given rise to the constant stream of attempts to identify points of transition, for Durkheim possessed a consummate ability to focus and refocus his arguments relative to specific tasks and to specific opponents. This completely bemused many of his critics. For instance, in replying to criticisms from Tarde in the second Preface, he admitted that there was no absolute definition of the social fact in his writings: 'All that matters is to select the characteristic which seems to suit best the purpose one has in mind. It is even highly possible to employ several criteria at the same time' (Durkheim, 1982: 43). This seems to be a key technique of Durkheim's work and it is important to note the way in which it is used. His arguments are pitched at a certain level of generality (he calls his concepts 'preliminary definitions'), and these approach the object from various directions, selecting appropriate characteristics. Now, together these definitions never make up a complete set, they may be supplemented. In some respects they resemble his lists of examples with which his methodological works are replete (which are examined in the next chapter) which he called 'incomplete inventories'. The dominance of the aim of the argument over its content is often so complete that apparently contradictory positions are adopted from text to text (e.g. the consideration of technical constraints in 1893 and 1894). This makes it difficult to identify serious shifts of theoretical posture.

Durkheim's 'initial inventory' is often presented as a simple itemisation of characteristics: 'there are these kinds of social facts', etc. But some characteristics are more inclusive than others; for example, he treats constraint as more general than moral obligation. The objective in 1888 and in 1894 was to define the social fact (and to identify a range of such facts); the aim in 1893 was to define the concept of the moral fact (and to identify a range). In his definition of the moral fact he sought to stress the necessity of the sanction and its predictability and he did this by emphasising the contingent nature of technical processes. The stick was bent in the other direction when it was necessary to stress the inevitability of the outcome when technical constraints were broken in defining social facts.

Again, the fact that Durkheim could extend the characteristics of the way social facts exert their powers, to include moral and intellectual prestige as opposed to obligation and sanction, shows how nimbly he was able to connect arguments about causation to his preliminary definitions. Obviously, different open sets of options could be connected with – or opposed to – others, in a practice which seemed always to have room for manoeuvre. But these texts, as if in a game of cards, play certain kinds of hands, and in order to master the way they are played it is important to know and understand the value of things and how they are calculated – a consideration which seems to have less to do with scientific proof than with the strategic operations relative to the goals of the programme itself.

There are, nonetheless, examples which seem to indicate not simply a change of focus but a development. One such case can be traced between the Introduction (1893) to the *Division* and the *Rules*: the rules relating to the distinction between normal and pathological phenomena.

NORMAL AND PATHOLOGICAL FACTS

In 1893 Durkheim attempted to define the normal *moral* fact relative to social type, and comparable phase of development, as 'every rule of conduct to which a repressive diffuse sanction is attached' (Durkheim, 1964b: 435). But where the evolution of the phenomenon in question is not sufficiently developed for the average society of the type to be determined with any degree of precision, difficulties present themselves. The situation of 'indecision', which characterises the advanced societies on the problem of normal moral development, can only be resolved through a more sophisticated application of the same method: the determination of the norm of well-being of the new state can only be reached through a knowledge of the previous one. If it can be shown that there is a 'functional identity' between the elements of the old and the elements of the new (resting on same causes, serving the same ends, having the same dependent structures) it must be normal, even though it cannot be established through comparison with the average case. The rule, to reiterate, is that such a moral fact is normal if it can be shown to be analogous to the former type.

In 1894 Durkheim tried once more to define the normal *moral* fact, and the method that must come into play where the average cannot be ascertained was altogether different. The 'external' index of the normal fact must be arrived at through knowledge of the average type, but proof of this relied on being able to show that the normal phenomenon was 'bound up with the conditions of existence of the species under consideration, either as a mechanically essential effect of these conditions or as a means for allowing the organism to adapt to these conditions' (Durkheim, 1982: 94). When the sociologist considered a complex transitional period it was vital that such structural analysis be undertaken, but it must never usurp the place of finding the norm through the average if this was at all possible. The reasons why this second method 'should in no case be substituted for the previous one, nor even be the first employed' (1982: 92) were numerous: causal structural analysis depended on the existence of firm and reliable facts already accumulated, and this was not the case in sociology; social forces may have improvised a remedy for an abnormality, and there was a danger that the sociologist take this as normal; there was also the danger that an immature functioning structure may be mistaken as norm yet the more effective forms might evolve. For all these reasons analysis must refuse to opt for premature analysis. So, in place of the supplementary rule that the normal can in some cases be found on the basis of analogies, this was changed in 1894 to:

one can verify the results of the preceding method [i.e., through the average] by showing that the generality of the phenomenon is bound up with the general conditions of collective life in the social type considered; this verification is necessary when this fact is related to a social species which has not yet accomplished its complete evolution. (1982: 97, mod)

The significance of this development in Durkheim's thought is that, compared with the definition of 1893, the second method is no longer seen as a simple extension of the first but is recognised as a method in its own right, even if it is presented as tempting the sociologist to an illegitimate short cut.

OBJECTIVITY

Another kind of development can also be seen between the writing of the 1893 Introduction to the *Division* and the *Rules*: the reorganisation of an argument, in this case the presentation of the basic thesis that the advance of social science depends upon adherence to the principle that the object of analysis must be treated 'as a thing'. In the second Preface (of 1901), Durkheim noted that many of the criticisms of rules

often arise from the fact that one has refused ... our basic principle, that of the objective reality of social facts. It is therefore upon this principle that in the end everything rests, and everything comes back to it. (Durkheim, 1982: 45)

The principles of objectivity, of causality, were, of course, announced in the earliest of Durkheim's writings, and certainly in his writings he insisted that it was not by starting from the idea of 'man' and deducing social characteristics that sociology could progress (e.g. Durkheim, 1964b: 421); nor could it progress if it was considered that society constitutes 'a world within a world, in which the laws of causality do not apply – in other words, it postulates a miracle' (Durkheim, 1978: 218).

But the emphasis on the external nature of social facts, and hence the failure of introspective methods, had led by 1893 only to the formulation that: 'the positive science of morality is a branch of sociology, for every sanction is principally a social thing' (Durkheim, 1964b: 428).

In fact, the general approach adopted to the conception of the nature of scientific method in the 1893 Introduction was completely dominated by reference to Descartes, not just an acknowledgment of the important principle of 'doubt' in a Cartesian sense, but also the requirement that

To subject an order of facts to science, it is not sufficient to observe them carefully, to describe and classify them, but what is a great deal more difficult, we must also find, in the words of Descartes, *the way in which they are scientific*, that is to say, to discover in them some objective element. (Durkheim, 1964b: 36–7)

In describing the problem of observation in this way the emphasis was placed on the search for a quality within the objects investigated.

But in the *Rules* Durkheim formulated the general rule that all social phenomena should be treated 'as things', and called this rule the fundamental rule of the objective method. The Cartesian principle of doubt was described as a negative application of the rule that insists on the necessity for the investigator to discard all 'prenotions', a term recovered from Bacon, which was then located as a corollary of the fundamental rule. Another corollary was announced as the need to select facts on the basis of an 'external characteristic' defined in advance: all phenomena so defined should be included in the group to be investigated on the basis of the rational consistency of definition. Durkheim's illustration of the consequences of not following this requirement, the conception of 'pseudo' crimes in the work of

Garofalo, came from the analysis in the *Division*. Only in the *Rules* was it argued that this principle was subordinate to the fundamental rule.

Thus two corollaries, one negative (abandon prenotions) and one positive (definitions must be based on selected 'external' characteristics), were dependent on the principle of objectivity established as the norm of scientific research. If in principle the movement of the basis of argument from Descartes to Bacon could give rise to certain problems in Durkheim's text, for the philosophies of the two philosophers were not identical, it is clear that for Durkheim's development there was no discontinuity. In 1893 Durkheim talked of 'laying aside' ready-made judgments, of 'putting aside' personal and subjective judgments, on the grounds that science requires 'complete freedom of mind' (1964b: 36–7); the terms in the *Rules* are exactly the same apart from the substitution of prenotion for 'ready-made judgment' (*jugements tout faits*). But in 1895 he seemed forced, as I have noted above, to write a special footnote to correct the balance of the argument, for the rules 'systematically discard prenotions' and 'select social facts defined in advance by an external objective characteristic' leaving the problem of how the sociologist was to begin any investigation except by producing new concepts out of nothing:

> It is in practice always the common concept and the common term which are the point of departure. Among the things that in a confused fashion this term denotes, we seek to discover whether any exist which present common external characteristics. (Durkheim, 1982: 84)

This tension seems to reflect an absence of a synthesis of the ideas of Descartes and Bacon, the removal of idolatry and the removal of *idola*. But it would be wrong, I think, to mistake this vacillation as indicative of a characteristic tendency to oscillate between alternatives. For the subordination of the Cartesian principle of doubt to the Baconian one of the systematic removal of prenotions is firmly established, for Durkheim obviously embraced both positions. The difficulty arises precisely in relation to how prenotions are to be removed: the 1895 note makes it clear that it is through rational redefinition and the creation of new terms that the sociologist will actually 'throw off the yoke of empirical categories'.

In sum, it is possible to begin to identify changes of focus (the movement from considerations of kinds of social facts); developments of the argument itself (the emergence of the complementary structural analysis of pathological formations); and the reorganisation of themes (the subordination of methodical doubt to the principle of the removal of prenotions).

14

An Examination of the Argument of the *Rules*

A method is justified only if it opens up a route.
(Mauss, 1979: 36)

At this point it is possible to pass from an investigation of the context of the *Rules* to an examination of the text itself.

DOMAIN

The very first sentence of Chapter One of the *Rules* suggests that method can only be applied to an object of study: and the discussion of the object of sociology could be regarded as not being, strictly speaking, a problem of method at all, but as an issue in theoretical construction. This seems to be confirmed in so far as the chapter works its way towards a definition of social facts rather than a methodological rule. It is clear, also, from Durkheim's earlier lectures, that the point at which the *Rules* begins is already a long way down the road that he had begun to travel. By omitting the presentation of the initial sociological problem, the opening chapter of the *Rules* very much gives the impression that it is simply a substitute for such theory, for it appears as the depiction of a terrain on which work prior to excavation can begin, rather than the auxiliary protocol to a specific sociological research programme linked to its political and theoretical sources.

Having chosen to apply the methods of the positive sciences (with all that implies) Durkheim immediately tackled the question of the subject matter of the new science in the light of the thesis that each science has its unique objects within which relations of causality exist;

like the others the social domain was a naturally emergent property, in this case of the associations between individuals. But given the fact that individuals have elements within them that are physical, biological, psychological and social, and that all these produce effects which combine together, the problem was how to locate the specifically social effects. Durkheim presented this issue as one of finding within social life phenomena that were supra-individual, that were as far as possible divorced from 'mixed' or 'combined' facts. He suggested, following the seventeenth century rationalists, that nature itself often produced phenomena of this type. But Durkheim posed the question directly to society: within social phenomena, there were also manifestations of the effects of natural causality. These could be grasped as the ways and degrees to which the free action of individuals were constrained. We can best follow Durkheim's exposition by looking at the way he illustrated his argument as it developed through the presentation of initial surveys of the field, or initial 'inventories' as he called them. Here I present the main inventories of Chapter One (against the paragraphs which I have enumerated from the 1982 translation (that of 1964a omits paragraph 14)).

1 *all individuals drink, sleep, eat, reason:* – these are not pure social facts, but an admixture of biological, psychological and social facts (para 2);

2 *domestic duties defined in law, custom, and sentiments derived from education; religious beliefs and practices; language; currency and credit; professional practices.* These are social facts which exist in a sense independently of the individual (para 4);

3 directly sanctioned forms: *law, moral rules, customs;* and indirectly constraining forms: *use of language, currency, technology.* Social facts exist independently and constrain the individual (para 5);

4 *political society and its religious, political, literary, and occupational subgroupings* are the social substratum not the individual; constraint can be normal or abnormal (para 6);

5 *waves of collective enthusiasm, indignation, pity, collective acts of atrocity:* it is difficult to realise these are also forms of constrained conduct (para 7);

6 *individuals eat, drink, sleep at regular hours and have a pattern of hygiene, courtesy, respect for traditions, etc.* which are social facts impressed by socialisation (para 8);

7 *formulas, legal rules and moral codes, aphorisms, maxims, articles*

of faith, literary forms: social facts exist in fixed forms even within the realm of social thought (para 9);

8 *marriage, suicide and birth rates* reflect currents of opinion which can be studied statistically (para 10);

9 (number and nature of social parts, their articulation, degree of coalescence) *population dispersal, extent and nature of communications, design of buildings, urbanisation, clothes* (paras 13–14): these 'fixed' facts are determined by moral currents, also have the characteristic of social facts, they constrain individual conduct, can be called 'morphological' facts;

10 *legal rule, moral maxim, professional custom, fashion:* there are gradations of the consolidation of 'physiological' facts. (para 16).

The structure of the argument is as follows: a) The definition of the domain of sociology requires an illustration of the problem of identifying pure social facts from mixed biological and psychological facts (1); the immediate evidence for the social fact is the existence of a range of human forms of conduct which are constrained either directly through sanctions or indirectly through the effect of the realities of the situation itself; (constraint can be normal or abnormal) (2–3). b) Social facts are ways of thinking and acting which exist 'independently' of each single individual, and do not have the individual as their immediate substratum, that is, their origins are within social relations; these collective forms are found in a continuum between stable or fixed kinds on the one hand and free-flowing ones on the other; they are general because social; generality, however, is not a sign that will guarantee the existence of social facts since there are mixed phenomena which are general, as well as biological facts which are general; yet the free-flowing currents are not inaccessible and can be studied through statistics; each collective form can and does have its own individual incarnations, and these too are recognisably distinct from the collective form proper (4–8); c) There are also social facts which are ways of being, which can be expressed in physical forms (9); but it should be remembered that ways of acting are also to be found in fixed forms (10). But as such, life and structure, organ and function differ only in degree not kind in the social domain.

There are two such general sets of conceptual oppositions which need to be examined separately: one concerns the level, the other the modality of the object.

PART THREE

Object of sociology: its generality
Now, there is an obvious difficulty stemming from the opposition
established between the social and individual throughout the
discussion, for they are in an important sense incommensurable: the
individual person is the product of a number of heterogeneous causes,
while the social is a phenomenon *sui generis*; great care has to be
exercised in consideration of the individual in this text – the objec-
tive/subjective opposition does not map exactly on to the soci-
al/individual one (para 4), 'the forms that ... collective states may
assume when they are refracted through individuals are things of a
different kind' (para 9), etc. Far from suggesting the individual is a
simple thing (a common charge against Durkheim), it is more complex
than society, and as such cannot be known directly; hence the need
for a complicated detour through sociology and psychology.

Modality of the object
The problem with the series of oppositions concerning the mode of
the object (physiology/morphology: acting/being: free/fixed current)
is that the terms do not match precisely (as is pointed out in paragraph
16 of the text). In the oppositions: life/structure; function/organ, etc.,
the constant image is that of free action as opposed to fixed structure;
the problem arises when Durkheim introduces a cross-cutting opposition: moral force/physical force (para 15: Nb 'social' should be
translated as 'moral', 4 lines up, 1982: 57), for then he has to add that
fixed forms exist within the physiological order (and presents 10),
with the result that the two orders appear to double the opposition
ideal/material. (This series of oppositions is so important it is necessary
to check this discussion with that found in Chapter Three. There the
identification of pathological forms is mapped onto the phy-
siology/morphology opposition to produce the opposition between
pathology of function /of structure (teratology).) In Chapter Five
we find further oppositions: things/persons; human/material milieux;
dynamic/physical density; material object/non-material object; mat-
ter/vital forces, etc. (Durkheim, 1982: 136–7). The basic proposition
here is that the general social milieu must be understood to involve a
specifically human milieu, which includes a 'physical concentration'
which is 'only the auxiliary element and almost invariably the consequence' of moral densities. But clearly Durkheim is consistent here,
for:

among 'things' must be included the products of previous social activity – the law and the customs that have been established, and literary and artistic monuments, etc.... to some extent they exert an influence upon social evolution whose rapidity and direction vary according to their nature. But they possess no elements essential to set that evolution in motion. (1982: 136 trans mod)

This certainly resolves the issue, for the products of currents of opinion, including traditions and the configuration of a communication system are both classed as the material things of the social milieu, to find themselves in opposition to the 'active factor', the 'human milieu' itself. This can be no other than the free current of social life acting on and against the 'things' of the physiological and morphological orders. The second Preface (of 1901) seems to confuse this by suggesting that 'social constraint' does not stem from the 'unyieldingness of certain patterns of molecules' and contrasts a moral with a physical milieu, but then makes the social object identical with representations which constrain through their authority and prestige. Even here there are significant caveats and qualifications: this formulation does not say that physical constraint does not exist in society; the phrase is as follows; 'what is exclusively peculiar to social constraint is that it stems ... from the prestige with which certain representations are endowed'; in other words, the formulation carefully avoids saying that social constraint is purely and directly ideal.

It is possible to check this reading against Durkheim's consideration of these issues made in 1897 (1970: 310–20), where he adds another rule, that the sociologist should not confuse the collective type and individual type (not just the individual level). The latter is produced by statistical averaging of individual phenomena; the social fact itself is qualitatively different (1970: 317).

OBJECTIVITY

Durkheim's discussion of 'rules for the observation of social facts' considers the position of sociology in the light of the already established scientific practices. The scientific revolution is conceived by Durkheim as having achieved a transformation of previous forms of thought in three ways. First, science regards the phenomena it studies as being a reality that is external to the mind of the observer, no part of which is unknowable in principle. Second, such external realities are 'represented in the mind' through sensations and concepts (Durkheim,

1982:60). In the process of the scientific revolution both sensations and concepts are transformed, but so too, and third, is the relation between them. Although all thought begins, in principle, from sensations, there is a tendency to invert the real order so that the object of thought comes to be seen as ideal and having its origins inside the mind. Science reverses this, and insists that the object must be studied as a thing which is outside the mind and independent from it. Durkheim's discussion of this transition and the way it can be fostered in sociology is made up of two parts: first an examination of the prescientific complex which he suggests is dominated by an 'ideological method'; and second, an elaboration of specific rules which must promote the development of scientific method in sociology at the level of concepts and the level of sensations. Here I will outline the main points of the argument, and then look at some of the difficulties which arise in the way that Durkheim presents them.

The most well-known part of Durkheim's argument is his attempt to argue that all knowledge stems from sensation; prescientific concepts are not judged in relation to their theoretical and epistemological adequacy but in relation to their practical adequacy: for example, in order to use the motion of the sun to make a division of the day that will serve as a clock it is not necessary to question the movement of the sun (1982:61). Concepts that are dominated by such practical concerns can be called, he said (following Bacon), 'prenotions', as opposed to scientific concepts. But at the root of these prenotions are sensations, which, in prescientific and purely practical knowledge, tend to be highly subjective and uncontrolled. (Thus this stage of knowledge is also called the 'subjective' stage (1982:71).) As empirical sensation does not act as a tight check on the elaboration of prenotions, these develop under the force of human desire as *Idola*, another Baconian term, which comes to stand for things as apprehended in sensation. This displacement is compounded because prenotions are also endowed with social prestige and authority, which makes it difficult for individuals to question their rationality (1982:63). The scientific project, then, seeks to replace subjective by objective measures of sensations, and *Idola* by rational concepts, so as to re-orient study from ideas to things.

Durkheim's rules call the sociologist 1. systematically to discard prenotions; 2. study phenomena grouped together by some external characteristic identified in advance; and 3. select for study social phenomena which appear most separated from any individual forms.

This combination of injunctions derives from the fundamental rules of objectivity. In discussing them Durkheim has often been accused of saying contradictory things, even that the rules are mutually exclusive. The charges are in fact linked: the call clearly states that, first, the sociologist discard prenotions and then, second, return to objective sensations in order to build scientific concepts; but Durkheim also says that in practice the task always begins with an examination of the adequacy of prenotions and that adequate terms may be developed through their redefinition. By ignoring the discussion of the second sociologists have been content to call the method 'crudely empiricist'; by taking the two together, others have called the method confused. Here I shall present the two formulations, and then examine the 'confusion'.

After demanding that 'one must systematically discard all prenotions', Durkheim says

> What has to be done is to form fresh concepts *de novo*, ones appropriate to the needs of science.... It is certainly not true that the commonly-held concept is useless. It serves as a benchmark ... it occasionally points to the approximate direction. (1982: 76)

At this point there is a footnote, added in 1895 to the first edition: 'It is in practice always the common concept and the common term which are the point of departure ...' (1982: 84). But the discussion in the main text continues, seven paragraphs later, to say:

> sociology, if it is to be scientific must start from sensation ... must create new concepts and to do so must lay aside common notions and the words used to express them, turning to sensations, the primary and necessary material of all concepts. It is from sensation that all general ideas are disengaged. (1982: 81 trans mod)

It seems to me that there is here a prime example of the way in which the writing of the *Rules* has created problems, for although in this chapter as a whole the position is balanced, in one or two places two quite separate and distinct theses begin to interfere with each other. One quite distinct thesis is that, in theory, all human knowledge has sensation as its basis; the other is that sociology must question prenotions and either correct them or replace them as it proceeds. But this latter thesis is often put in the strongest manner, that sociology should dispense altogether with them, and is then joined with the idea that all knowledge comes from sensation directly, and so sociology 'disengage' from objective sensations the elements for new concepts.

The note Durkheim attached in 1895 is the most balanced formulation:

> It is in practice the common concept and the common term which are the point of departure. Among the things that in a confused fashion this term denotes, we seek to discover whether any exist which present common external characteristics. If there are any, and if the concept formed by grouping the facts brought together in this way coincides, if not entirely (which is rare) but at least for the most part, with the common concept, it will be possible to continue to designate the former by the same term... But if the difference is too considerable, the creation of new and special terms becomes a necessity. (1982: 84)

What is outlined, then, is a demand concerning the radical empirical origin of knowledge and a *reform in the way concepts are organised*. But this resolves one problem and points to the complexity of the other, for here Durkheim indicates that by sensation he means a certain kind of raw material. From the way that the argument of the chapter is organised it is clear that the third rule (the corollary that the sociologist choose a certain kind of phenomena for study) is posed in this scheme at the level of the observation of sensation, i.e., comparable with the way natural sciences have sought radically new forms of evidence, using completely new instruments.

As I have shown in the previous chapter, it is precisely this third corollary which was rewritten in the 1895 version – from a call to study first social facts that were most consolidated, to one concentrating on those social facts most separated from individual forms. The whole of the argument when first constructed then, in 1894, identified the issue of the objective measurement of sensation with access to the social facts possessing the greatest natural objectivity: 'a sensation is more objective the more stable the object to which it relates' (1982: 82 trans mod). That Durkheim could have had in his mind a study of suicide rates when he wrote this formulation in 1894 is certainly inconceivable. He provided a list of examples in the text: study solidarity through legal rules; the family through the legally established right of succession; popular beliefs through proverbs; etc. (1982: 83). This enables Durkheim to discuss the proposition that facts of law, of punishment, are external sensations which can be seen to give the social scientist a privileged route to the study of social things. The argument in the 1895 version manages to imply the parallel between quantitative measurement in the natural sciences (new instrumentation) as a sensory contact with things, and social statistics as a sensory contact with social things.

(The emphasis on the study of consolidated, fixed social facts is an extension of the latter idea, indicated in the terms Durkheim uses for the whole chapter – on the 'observation' of social facts and their definition through 'visible' external characteristics, however super-ficial.) Thus Durkheim does not argue that sociology studies the external world directly, nor that the information produced at this level is somehow natural: science immediately demands a *reform in the way sensations are produced* and selected just as concepts require redefinition. What is essential to his position, and indeed all non-idealist positions, is that these sensations are different from, indeed situated at a different level from, prenotions or concepts, i.e., not ideas. They are none the less the primary material in relation to which ideas must be formed.

PATHOLOGY

Having in the first section of the *Rules* suggested that social facts must be conceived as external to the individual, and in the second that the sociologist must study certain of their external characteristics, in the third section of the book Durkheim outlines rules for classifying them in order to begin to analyse their internal reality. In a previous chapter I have examined the way in which the development of Durkheim's ideas on the divisions between normal and pathological phenomena involved the construction of two different – even opposed – metho-dological procedures. In the *Rules* of 1894 this had become established as a division between a rule which defined normality in relation to the average member of a social species, and another which arrived at a definition via an analysis of the apparent relationship between the generality of the fact and the 'general conditions of collective life' in the society under consideration.

But Durkheim's discussion of the rules for drawing the line between normal and pathological phenomena has been the most disturbed by the waywardness of translators. Even the recent (1982) translation makes serious errors (normal for abnormal (p. 98), and confusions over terms such as morbidity, abnormality, teratology, etc.), but then it must be admitted that Durkheim changed his mind on some of these formulations himself between 1893–4 (e.g. *maladie* into *anomalie*, etc.; and added numerous supplementary notes – numbers 1, 4, and extended 13; and added note 15 in 1901). And the style of the writing has been justly criticised; it seems to have been written in great haste.

The argument is, however, clear. The order of the argument moves from a discussion of the vital connection between theory and action and how the distinction between normal and pathological facts facilitates rational practice, through a definition of normal social facts, to an illustration of the immediate and dramatic implications of this definition for the understanding of even the most vital of social phenomena. He criticises two possible definitions: pathology is signalled when pain is present (this is discounted on the grounds that some pain seems normal, e.g. the pain of childbirth), or normality is a 'perfect adaptation to the environment' (which is rejected theoretically and as totally impractical in sociology). His attempt to resolve the issue follows the pattern of attempting to find an external but objective sign for normality. This can be found, he suggests, through the conception of the average or generic type of social species, by assembling 'in one entity the most frequently occurring characteristics' (1982: 91). This would be different from an 'individual' type, and would approach the norm for the species at a given phase in its development. It can be assumed, following the biological sciences, that variations from the normal are not contingent, but have specific causes; this requires the establishment from the beginning of a whole branch of special study. The discussion of the theoretical issues raised here is cut short here, and Durkheim launches into an examination of the effects of the definition.

Before turning to this, it is important to note the unfortunate break in this discussion at this point, for Durkheim had used in the *Division* and was about to use in *Suicide* some important techniques for examining these problems, developed in part from German psychological theory (Weber and Fechner). The development of the analysis of anomie, egoism and altruism, for example, used the framework of normal thresholds. Far from positing, at this stage, a different register of pathological causation, the analysis unified normal and abnormal phenomena via a theory of the effects of the whole social form on its internal tendencies by tracing the movement of the equilibration of contradictory currents.

But without introducing this theoretical analysis, Durkheim claimed that the new definition was far from being a simple 'logical formalism' for 'even the most essential facts totally change their character' in the light of its application (1982: 103). Take crime, for example; when the rule is applied, it is clear, since crime is found in all societies and rates of crime and types of crime vary with different social types, it must be a normal social fact. If it was normal it was certain that there was something about crime which contributed to social well-being, and which in turn led to its reproduction. Durkheim remarked that the conclusion was so unexpected and out of line with prevailing opinion that he had initially rejected it himself, before reflection on the reasons why it might indeed be the case. If the causes of crime do not lie in the tendencies of individuals who commit them, then in a sense they are just as much the victims of society's own needs. But if this was the conclusion reached by the application of the rule to crime, it did not produce, of itself, an answer to the question of whether the rate of crime was abnormal: on this Durkheim was content to say, in a note added in 1901, that his suspicion was that in the modern crisis, there were abnormally high rates, but 'on this matter one can only hypothesize' (1982: 107).

But the analysis of crime is important in the sense that, in his opposition to the Italian criminologist Garafalo, Durkheim was able to illustrate, concretely, two major features of the new method: first the way in which the role of rational definitions functioned (for Durkheim sought not an essential definition, though dialectic, but a characteristic 'external sign' for the existence of crime, which he found in the presence and action of sanctions) and in the rational distinction between normal and abnormal moral facts. (Durkheim sought the further objective sign of the appearance of the phenomena in the generic type.) Failure to use these methods had serious consequences: it was responsible for the prevailing misconception that crime rates are solely produced out of the personal characteristics of the criminals, and the utopian view that society could through an act of will eliminate crime from its domain (see 1982: 78–9, 103).

CAUSES

From the middle sections of the book the discussion changes emphasis somewhat, from the need to define 'external' characteristics of social facts, etc. to the requirement of experimental science. For example, even in the consideration of the construction of social classification the preferred method is that of experiment, not that of accumulation of evidence. Again Durkheim makes a direct appeal to Bacon: it is not quantity of facts that is important but their quality. Even the quantitative concept of generality is then subordinated:

In order to know whether a fact is general throughout a particular species it will be unnecessary to have observed all societies belonging to this species.... In many cases even one observation well conducted will be enough, just as often one experiment efficiently carried out is sufficient to establish a law. (1982: 110–1)

All the elements of research strategy are bent to the requirements of crucial experiments. But the problem is that the selection of material which is most directly relevant to the study of the most important aspects of the phenomena under investigation may only be possible when the analysis of the facts is 'sufficiently advanced' (1982: 111). As he had mentioned in respect of economics (1982: 68), even the introduction of theory can be achieved only at a certain point in the development of a discipline, for it is not in relation to the quantity of facts but of progress in theory which demands a different kind of fact. Progression at the empirical level goes hand in hand with the development of theory: 'These two parts of science are linked, depending on each other for progress' (1982: 111, mod).

How are social facts to be accounted for? Here Durkheim returns to the problem of the conception of what a society is, the emergence of social realities as products of individual association (he gives further inventories of the action of the social on the individual (1982: 130)), this time to investigate not the definition of the social fact itself but the order of causal primacy. I have already referred to this discussion earlier in the chapter. Here I want to clarify the issue of this order more carefully. Durkheim specifies the order as follows: social facts are to be explained by social facts not individual ones; and social functions contribute to a social end not individual ones. Of the two main aspects of society, its volume and its 'dynamic density', it is the latter which contains the motor element of social development; dynamic density is made up of two forces: a physical which 'influences', and a moral density which determines social change (1982: 136).

It may at first sight seem paradoxical that Durkheim should, after defining the order in this way, suggest that social classification must be accomplished through the appeal to the principle of morphology. The reason for this is that the facts of morphology play 'a preponderant role', and the 'origin of social processes' must be sought in the 'constitution' of the inner social milieu formed of morphological (i.e. anatomical) elements. But it is clear that the whole line of argument in support of the principle is consistent with the choice of such an index, while holding to the view that the main force is 'moral concentration, of which physical concentration is only the auxiliary element, and almost invariably the consequence' (1982: 136).

To reach a position in sociology where it is possible to invoke these principles means to engage first of all in genuine experimentation. The primary aim of the comparative method, so conceived, is to be able to discover two facts which 'accompany or exclude each other externally', at least as regards 'quantitative aspects' (1982: 151). The search for correspondences of this kind is still posed in terms of the primacy, at this stage, of the exterior face of objects, the immediately given. Out of these it is necessary to find the elements to form comparisons. A whole paragraph was added to the 1895 edition to strengthen this idea:

> To illustrate an idea is not to prove it. What must be done is not to compare isolated variations, but a series of variations, systematically constituted, whose terms are correlated with each other in as continuous a gradation as possible.... (1982: 155)

Far from indicating superficial connections, these are regarded as the essential route to scientific 'interpretation'.

The overall strategy of the *Rules* resolves itself quite simply: the definition of orders of social facts facilitates the discovery of possible series of covariation of phenomena selected from these orders. The route to the discovery of the internal connections is still a matter of further 'elaboration'. But this process is almost left as a secondary issue. As an example, Durkheim leaves the reader with an interesting example:

> It can be established absolutely certainly that the tendency to suicide varies according to education. But it is impossible to understand how education can lead to suicide ... thus we are moved to ask whether both facts might not be the consequence of one single state. This common cause is the weakening of religious traditionalism, which reinforces at the same time the desire for knowledge and the tendency to suicide. (1982: 152–3)

Durkheim's thesis on the phases of scientific development can be summarised as follows:

Phase one is characterised by logical rational reforms working on the external or superficial surface of reality: it attempts to adopt the scientific mentality, to establish rational definitions and new instruments for the production of empirical material which make contact with things in a new way. The results can be seen immediately in that, even working with inadequate data, certain new interpretations can be undertaken – for example the rational application of the rules for determining the normal and the pathological reveals the normality of crime in society, etc.

Phase two is dominated by the formation of laws through experimentation, and their interpretation. The activity is not dominated by work on superficial characteristics, it is able to penetrate these and to establish a knowledge of the internal connections between things. Thus at this stage it would be possible to move from an analysis of the formal identification of the fact of the universal feature of crime in society, to the identification of the actual pathological rate of crime in any one case and its determinants.

15

Criticisms of Durkheim Examined

Having clarified the argument of the *Rules* and established something of the character of the way it was written, it is now possible to test the major criticisms against the logic of Durkheim's methodological position. Hence what is proposed is in no sense an exhaustive assessment of the range of criticisms, but to try to use this partial assessment as a way of investigating the subtlety of Durkheim's position.

(i)

Firstly, it is evident that some of the most important problems raised in interpretation stem from the mode of argumentation adopted by Durkheim (I have alluded to some of them already, particularly the problems in the text which arise from the rewritings of 1895). Also over Durkheim's arguments against adversaries or contrary positions which sometimes become unbalanced and, if the arguments does not contextualise, give rise to one sided interpretations (the fraught issue of empiricism is one example but there are many others, e.g. over his anti-historicism in Chapter 5). But there is a fundamental problem around which many of the others revolve, which may be located in the first chapter. It is an exemplary feint and has become the basis of a whole tradition of (mis)interpretation. Durkheim, astonishingly perhaps, said he could not have imagined how such an interpretation could have been extracted (Durkheim, 1982: 43). In a sense, however, one definition of the social fact presented could only lead to the meaning said to be unintended. The issue of the 'imputed' thesis is only one element of the extraordinary fascination which the first chapter exercises: it is not a simple statement of intent, a call to work. It has become a captivating, logical maze.

I have presented, already, a brief synopsis and a critical look at the first chapter with its labyrinth of oppositions (life/structure; organ/function; general/particular; objectivity/subjectivity; external/internal; etc.), and I have suggested that a key problem is the way in which these terms form an asymmetrical totality. I have also noted the problems which have arisen, more fundamentally, from the way that this chapter has been detached from the framework of theoretical problems established in other works, so that the chapter seems to work towards the delineation of a unique domain of facts, not towards an answer to problems posed in sociological analysis. But if we turn now to investigate how this aim is achieved, not simply in terms of the sets of conceptual oppositions but of broader techniques of argument, the analysis of how the complexities have been constructed and written enables us to pose the important question as to how misconceptions have arisen. I will use this example to lead in to a discussion of charges that Durkheim's work is logically flawed, substantialist, inconsistent, empiricist, and entails a narrow conception of the individual.

(ii)
Let us look again at the elements combined in the first chapter. Its objective is presented immediately in the question: 'What is a social fact?' Durkheim answers this through an analogy with the existing sciences: each has its unique field of objects corresponding to the hierarchy of the emergent properties of nature. The social domain, he suggests, is an emergent property of the association of individuals (this argument, far from being a simple prop, can be seen to have a range of vital theoretical functions); nevertheless, this does not mean that individuals, as such, form the social substratum (the matrix of the emergent phenomenon itself fulfils this role). But social facts are 'reflected' or 'incarnated' in individuals, and in so doing they merge into complex 'mixed' phenomena (deriving from physical, chemical, biological, psychical, social causes). Sociology establishes, then, an overturning, a 'reversal' of normal perceptions, for the proposition is developed that the social order is qualitatively different and thus superior to the individual and 'dominates (the individual) infinitely' (Durkheim, 1953: 57). Two possible definitions of the social fact are proposed: as ways of acting which exert external constraints on the

'individual', or, as general ways of acting which exist in collective forms separate from any of the individual forms in which they might be realised. These definitions apply different criteria, said Durkheim, either singly or in combination (reflecting the complexity of the hierarchy of logical oppositions). But two further arguments are reflected in these definitions. One is the thesis of the causal primacy of the motive forces of the social whole indeed seen as *causa sui* (developed in a set of terms in which the aspect of determinancy experienced as necessity is invoked – pressure, constraint, obligation, etc.); the other is the thesis of the methodological order or investigation, of finding, first, 'external' or objective signs to identify the existence of social phenomena (developed in terms in which the aspect of objectivity is invoked – material consolidation, stability, generality, fixity, etc.).

In the presentation of the exposition the two theses fulfil different functions: one leads to the idea that what constitutes social facts is that they are 'beliefs, tendencies and practices of the group taken collectively' (Durkheim 1982: 54), the other to the idea that it is possible to recognise them 'through their power of external coercion' (1982: 56). So, it may appear that the second thesis interferes with the first, in fact usurps the role of the first. For, instead of either defining the social fact through an analysis of the way in which it is a phenomenon *sui generis*, or concluding that such social facts can be selected on the basis of applying an analogy (such phenomena can be recognised by the characteristic traits of externality and objectivity), he reaches a 'definition' of the social fact, and the domain of sociology, which has substituted the sign for the content.

There are different remedies suggested in Durkheimian criticism to correct this error: one, suggested by Lacombe (1926), is that one of the definitions (suggesting external constraint) is linked with a whole thesis of social consciousness (the *conscience collective*) which needs to be removed altogether from Durkheimian sociology if it is to progress. Another, suggested by Lukes among others, is that the formulation should simply be redefined to clear up a mistake in the conception:

Durkheim should have said that they are both external to and internal to (that is, internalised by) any given individual; and that they are only external to all existing individuals in so far as they have been culturally transmitted to them from the past. (Lukes, 1973: 12)

But there is another possibility, of course, in line with Durkheim's own view: the first step of unravelling this feint, it could be suggested, would be to relocate the argument first with respect to the sociological problem, and secondly with respect to method, since the basic methodological problem it raises is actually subordinate to the provisional recognition and observation of social phenomena (at an early stage of analysis). The first chapter then, it would appear, does not answer one question so dramatically posed, of 'What is a social fact?' It also answers a secondary question: how can social facts be recognised? It remains to be seen whether the answer to the second question contains itself a general theory of the social fact.

There are many diverse aspects to this issue, for it raises theoretical, logical, epistemological and substantive problems in Durkheim's sociological practice. From the point of view of the discussion here it is most convenient to begin with the logical question, as this will enable us to set out the main agenda of problems.

The logical problem can be specified most readily through an examination of the complex relations and differences between the two definitions of the social fact which Durkheim reaches at the end of Chapter One. (A social fact is any way of acting, fixed or not, capable of exerting over the individual an external constraint, *or* which is general over the whole of a given society whilst having an existence of its own, independent of its individual manifestations.) The lucid simplicity of such definitions is a characteristic mark of Durkheim's writing, but so also is its actual complexity. If we analyse these definitions we find 1. two main elements – ways of acting/individual; 2. a specification of the character of ways of acting (fixed-fluid, or general); and 3. a specification of the character of the relation between the two main elements (external, constraining, or independent). But the 'individual' is not the same in the two definitions, a fact linked to the two conflicting aims of the chapter (one of which appeals directly to the reader as an individual who experiences constraints, and the other, which is at one stage removed, and refers to individual manifestations or forms).

What Durkheim never imagined could be 'imputed' to him (Durkheim, 1982: 43) was the interpretation that the sign of constraint could be understood as explaining the nature of the social fact. After the *Rules* he constantly reiterated his view that what was intended was to identify a mark by which such phenomena may be recognised and grouped together: thus what is at issue is the conception of (i) the function of the definition and (ii) the theoretical content of the definition. In order to answer these questions it is useful to examine what alternatives Durkheim had before him, without saying what he should have said (Lukes has provided such an alternative); but there are several others which could have been produced from the diverse discussion of Chapter One. Instead of saying 'ways of action', 'collective form or genre' could have been used; instead of 'external constraint', 'direct or indirect coercive power', or even 'ways of acting or being to which we are obliged to conform' (cf., 1975:i,102); or the formula – forms of collective activity whether 'ideal or physical' to which the individual accedes 'knowingly or unknowingly'. All these are among the various possibilities which the material allows, and there are others which Durkheim constructed at different stages of his career as I have quoted in an earlier chapter. What is surprising is that Durkheim not only admitted this selectivity, it was he said, *an essential technique of his approach:* 'all that matters is to select the characteristic which seems to suit best the purpose one has in mind ... it is ... possible to employ several criteria at the same time according to circumstances' (Durkheim, 1982:43). 'Characteristic' here can be any way in which the phenomenon appears to the observer whose selection reflects the application of a relevant 'criterion': 'a principle' (e.g. his sociology is in part the application of the spiritualist principle), or an 'analogy' (the application of the dichotomy morphology/physiology), etc.

If Durkheim's work is characterised by such accumulations of diverse perspectives the problem of the logical structure of the argument is clarified: heterogeneous characteristics may be selected, and heterogeneous criteria may be applied in the analysis, criteria which may be cross-cutting, or be posed at different levels of generality (e.g. individual as opposed to individual manifestation of social facts, ideational as opposed to functional principles, etc.). But the possibility of the existence of alternative objectives in the discussion also contributes to the complexity. It seems that the different levels of the discussion might well be related to these aims: the identification of 'ways of acting' (etc.) is different from that of 'collective forms', just as that of 'the individual' is different from that of 'individual forms' of the social fact, just as identification of social causes is different from that of social influences. If Durkheim wanted to say something about what a social fact might be, then concepts which specified their *sui generis* nature were required. Given that he had specified the 'individual' is to be thought of as a complex resultant (a mixed fact), and constituted something of an obstacle to sociology in its early stages, research should centre where the *causa sui* was, in principle, most clearly active, i.e., in most evidently delineated collective formations themselves. We find this issue dealt with in the first chapter, in the discussion of the basic matrix of the social fact, the association of individuals as a *sui generis* productive mechanism: of new phenomena and of new sources of social energy, and this latter aspect of the argument could also have figured in the definition. It does figure indirectly, for what Durkheim has attempted to imply in giving primacy to the social over the individual, is also its unique coercive power. Thus the primacy of the social fact over the individual was not simply a logical one.

Before returning to this logical problem, I will examine the first of a number of fundamental charges against Durkheim's formulations.

(iii)

In order to examine the charge that Durkheim's conception of the social fact is substantialist it will help if we now turn to look in more detail at Durkheim's conception of the social totality. It can now be seen that a number of his most significant points come together here: 1. the idea that a simple totality contains no component parts (1982: 113); 2. that a complex totality is made of parts; 3. that it is of an irreducible complexity and cannot be explained by referent to any of its elements taken in isolation; 4. that its existence is also held to be conditional (raising the problem of its limits, thresholds); 5. that its complexity itself, in this perspective, is also something that evolves (leading to a division between primary and derived social facts), a development which can be studied comparatively and historically. The fundamental idea, however, is that the whole is more than the sum of its parts (Durkheim, 1982: 128), and, specifically, that society is more than the sum of its individual members (1982: 129).

Certain alternative, simplistic and idealist concepts of the totality are always targets for criticism in Durkheim's work and comparisons of Durkheim's principle with them are instructive. For Descartes 'there was nothing real ... apart from uniform, homogeneous, geometrical extension. As for the innumerable properties of which life is composed, the individuality of things, he sees them as mere appearances, tricks of light and shade.' Under this influence, he continues, 'how could a sense of diversity and complexity fail to be eradicated' (Durkheim, 1977: 275–6). Every time, virtually, that Descartes' name is mentioned this theme is discussed. Another object of constant criticism is the Leibnizian conception of the pre-established 'providential' harmony of the whole, a position which is mentioned in the *Rules* itself (e.g. Durkheim, 1982: 121).

Many commentators have concluded, however, that Durkheim's conception of the social whole is of an 'expressive' type, either taking and using the Althusserian term (Althusser and Balibar, 1970: 186) explicitly (e.g. Hirst, Lacroix, Filloux, Besnard) or developed in parallel formulations (e.g. Gurvitch). Actually, of course, this objection follows somewhat in the tradition of Tarde, who argued that Durkheim's conception of the whole was simply a vitalist and realist substantialism, a charge answered many times in Durkheim's work and even in the *Rules* (Durkheim, 1982: 141). In *Suicide* he said

> there is some superficiality about attacking our conception as scholasticism and reproaching it for assigning to social phenomena a foundation in some vital principle or other of a new sort.... There is nothing substantival or ontological about (the social) substratum, since it is a whole composed of parts. (1970: 319)

Durkheim's conception explicitly formulates: one cannot explain 'the whole by the part' ('materialist metaphysics') just as

> one cannot, following idealist and theological metaphysics, derive the part from the whole, since the whole is nothing without the parts which form it.... We must then explain phenomena that are the product of the whole by the characteristic properties of the whole, the complex by the complex.... (Durkheim, 1953: 29, orig. 1898)

But there might be other sources for appearance of the vitalist substance or essence in the theory: the conception of social energy and social forces (perhaps connected with the idea of the social Being). If this were to be the case, Durkheim's thought would contain an immense irony, for the critique in the *Rules* of inadequate conceptions of cause, of time, of social force, etc., is based on the view that they are constituted by an illegitimate application of principles from a naive psychology. Indeed, even at the point Durkheim refers to the emergent qualities of the social as in a sense forming a new individuality, a new 'being', he inserted, on reflection in 1895, a new footnote warning that this was not to be read as indicating some 'hypostatisation' of the *conscience collective*, it was to draw a demarcation line between two different orders by providing two quite separate terms for them (Durkheim, 1982: 129, 145).

Let us turn for a moment to another way of looking at this issue, to the notoriously difficult relation between individual action and social causation. It is fundamental to Durkheim's position that the two are not only profoundly different in principle but they must be held apart in any sociological analysis. This creates very interesting problems in the *Rules* which are rarely noticed, for the 'individual' as such does of course appear as a real entity, and Durkheim is keen to retain the term for a variety of reasons.

Obviously, Durkheim is adamant that the 'determining cause' of a social fact must not be sought 'among the states of the individual consciousness' (Durkheim, 1982: 134). However, the problem does not really end there for the action of the individual on social facts is manifestly admitted:

Psychical phenomena can only have social consequences when they are so closely linked to social phenomena that the actions of both are necessarily intermingled. This is the case for certain socio-psychical phenomena. Thus a public official is a social force, but at the same time he is an individual. The result is that he can employ the social force he commands in a way determined by his individual nature and thereby exerts an influence on the constitution of society. This is what occurs with statesmen and, more generally, with men of genius. The latter, although they do not fulfil a social role, draw from the collective sentiments of which they are the object an authority which is itself a social force, one which they can to a certain extent place at the service of their personal ideas. But it can be seen that such cases are due to individual chance and consequently cannot affect the characteristics which constitute the social species, which alone is the object of science. (1982: 145–6)

This idea goes back to the beginnings of Durkheim's work, but it is in the *Division* that a related formulation can be found, even presented as a rule, one of many not directly incorporated into the *Rules*:

Whenever we find ourselves in the presence of a governmental system endowed with great authority, we must seek the reason for it, not in the particular situation of the governing, but in the nature of the societies they govern. We must observe the common beliefs, the common sentiments which by incarnating themselves in a person or family, communicate such power to it. As for the personal superiority of the chief, it plays only a secondary role in the process ... if such superiority suggests the sense in which the current is directed, it does not create the current. (Durkheim, 1964a: 196)

The concept of 'power' is located at the level of the analysis of social forces, a theme continued directly in the *Elementary Forms* (see Lacroix, 1979). The very widespread view that Durkheim did not have a concept of power (which one can still find in Lukes's introduction to the new translation of the *Rules*) would certainly have been dispelled had Durkheim included this formulation into the *Rules* itself. Power is the effectivity which results from the harnessing of social forces (1961: 221ff).

Nevertheless one thing is clear: Durkheim distinguishes between the determining cause of social facts and elements which may 'influence' the way that society is constituted.

It seems that there are a number of deeper lying principles here which are not spelt out in the texts.

In order to investigate this further, let us examine a different example: in Rome if the father of a family enjoys absolute power, it is not 'because he is the oldest or wisest, or the most experienced, but because, according to the circumstances in which the Roman family was placed, he incarnated the old familial communism' (Durkheim, 1964a: 196). Many other instances could be cited. In Durkheim's sociology of religious entities, the Gods grow more powerful as society itself develops its capacities. Collective forces are primary here, the form of the representation secondary.

Collective representations thus have energy concentrated in them. Energy is generated by a variety of social mechanisms, the most important of which are collective gatherings which are the bases of collective effervescence. There are also pathological political forms, e.g. tyrannies have abnormal power because the structure of countervailing social forces is enfeebled; the individual can 'harness' these forces, not create or destroy them; these forces are created and modified by society as a whole (its size, its centres of moral interactions, etc.). Under some circumstances these forces are represented as anonymous, in others they are hypostatised; in some made the concrete, in others the abstract object of religious veneration. Durkheim's theory of ideology intervenes significantly at this point. For in pre-scientific modes of representation of these forces are operative all the elementary conceptions of cause and effect. Indeed, it is precisely in the substantialist idea that the fundamental principle of the unities and divisions of clan, lineage and tribal societies – blood – produces its magical but decisive effects. In the final formulations of religious (causal) theory, in societies where individualisation was already highly developed, the individual came to be regarded as a vital empirical moment in the social complexity, giving rise to the illusion (in Pascal) of the contradiction between body and soul (an illusion Durkheim thought sociology could dispel, since the religious idea of such totalities was still based on simplistic idealist assumptions (Gane, 1983a; 1983b).)

But the links between the individual and assumptions about causal social relations raise other important questions which should be considered here.

(iv)
Durkheim thus tries to think out the consequences of analysing the idea of social force through the way it makes its appearance in everyday life. This obviously creates difficulties for the reader, since Durkheim follows this through a number of important steps: social facts can only be explained by other social facts and not by the averaged or accumulated effects of actions of individuals. By attempting to work by analogy with individual activity, sociology would reproduce the illusions created by the apparent volitional freedom and efficacity of the subject as uniquely free of structural determinations. Yet the human subject acts only in a limited and particular sphere (Durkheim, 1982: 55–6) and cannot perceive directly the action of deeper and wider determinations. The appeal to psychology must be resisted, and Durkheim elaborates a number of critical precautions. A principal idea here is the thesis that there is a difference between the historical sequence of the appearance of social facts and their real causal relation; there is also implied a notion of the difference between the functional coexistence of social facts and their causal relation; and further, that social facts are caused both by society and by products of society, that social facts themselves are causal and conditional, etc. These are used to counter the view that sociology can be developed through the direct application of principles derived from an individualistic conception of human nature to social nature (1982: 128).

If the emphasis here can be seen to be firmly placed on thinking at the level of the structure of the whole, this should not be read as if Durkheim adopted a simplistic attitude to the study of the individual. Tarde jumped to this conclusion, just as writers like Ricoeur did later, who suggested that sociology lacked a phenomenological conception of individual psychology, and so illegitimately inserted the force of the *representations collective* into a naturalist psychology, so that social forces are thought to wrestle mechanically against vital individual tendencies (Ricoeur, 1949: 118). The impression of social life which Durkheim presents to certain readers is that of a mystical but objective social whole resting on, intervening in, struggling against, a mass of individuals conceived as being in complete and mechanical uniformity. This misreading has persisted, although Durkheim went to great lengths to dispel it by insisting on the difference between the 'individual', the 'individual type', the 'average individual', even in his conception of 'mechanical solidarity', stressing the complexity of the realities at this level (while holding to the view that societies were infinitely more complex (Durkheim, 1982: 131) to show two qualitatively different phenomena).

For Durkheim, then, the sociologist must be able to suspend the immediate judgment concerning humanist assumptions of the nature of individual psychology, i.e., it is not at all necessary to develop an elaborate individual psychology or hermeneutics as a precondition or as a starting point for sociology. He recognised that this was a difficult suspension, and emphasised that there were considerable obstacles for sociologists to overcome in order to practise it in a society with strong individualistic currents in its culture. Nevertheless, it is a precondition for the consideration of truly social causation. Durkheim emphasised that, whereas an education in psychology (which he himself actually taught of course), 'constitutes a necessary propaedeutic for the sociologist . . . it can only be of service to him if . . . he frees himself from it, going beyond it' (1982: 135 mod).

But in the advanced societies with their religions of the individual (themselves social forces) the evident reality of empirical individual, historical and biographical procession, linked with the illusion of the omnipotence of individual will, produced the notion that explanations must follow the linear temporal sequence of continuous social action, as this is the way individuals act and create larger social relations. This is often accompanied by another simplistic assumption: that analysis should trace a phenomenon back to its most simple and original state, so that the historical analysis can follow the flow of a history which witnesses the creation of the complex by the accumulation of simple elements or actions. Durkheim's response was to oppose such ideas by developing methodological constraints, linked to such anti-historicist ideas as 'the stages which humanity successively passes do not engender each other' (1982: 139), which is the basis for the proposition that societies of the segmental type do not create societies of the organised type (a principal idea of the *Division*). Durkheim constantly reiterated that the advanced societies have not the elementary societies as their cause, for they cause themselves *causa sui*. However, they do not make themselves out of nothing, and the materials carry something of their origins with them (they cannot be absolutely transformed, not because they contain an immutable

essence, a very widely held misinterpretation, but because their reproduction rests on mechanisms which are not absolutely transformed;
their causes never cease completely to operate). The same principle
can be seen discussed in other texts. When *Educational Thought* is
read closely, the propositions developed do rely on the assumption that
while 'society' or 'religion' or 'education' does not have an absolute
beginning or any first cause, it is true that they can have an historical
beginning, a formative period in which a 'first' causal complex is at
work. At another level, to take the theme of *Elementary Forms*, it is
true that as religions become more complex in social evolution 'it is
undeniably possible to arrange them in a hierarchy' since the differences
are not of kind and are not 'sufficient to place the corresponding
religions in different classes' (1961: 15), there is something which can be
identified by very general characteristics as 'religion'. The elementary
forms are manifestly less complex than the later formations so
'undoubtedly we can only touch very elementary facts by this method
... the novelties of every sort which have been produced in course
of evolution will not yet be explained' (Durkheim, 1961:21). This
fundamental orientation can be compared with the rationale for the
study of educational history:

> The present is composed of an infinite number of elements which are so
> closely intertwined that it is difficult for us to see clearly where one begins
> and another ends.... By direct scrutiny we can only arrive at a very crude
> and confused conception. The only way in which we can distinguish and
> analyse these elements ... is by carrying out historical research into the manner
> whereby they have progressively come to cluster together, to combine and
> form organic relationships.... (Durkheim, 1977: 15)

(And see the same argument made for the 'historical' study of the
family in 1888 (Durkheim, 1978: 211).)

But does not this confuse the relation of statics (*circumfusa*) and
dynamics (*praeteria*)? The translations of the *Rules* do not help here.
The second translation introduces an editorial insertion of what is
intended as a clarification (after the word *circumfusa*), clearly, from
the argument, it refers not to influences but the causal social milieu *at
a given moment*), the

> conception of the social environment as the determining factor in collective
> evolution is of the greatest importance. For if it is discarded, sociology is
> powerless to establish any causal relationship ... the external environment
> ... can only make its influence felt through the mediation of the internal
> social environment. The principal causes of historical development would not

therefore be found among the *circumfusa* (external influences). They would be found in the past . . . and sociological explanations would consist exclusively in linking the present to the past. (Durkheim, 1982: 139)

Davy also imagined that the distinction between *circumfusa* and *preterition* was utterly confused (in Durkheim, 1957: xxxi). But Durkheim's close colleagues were not only very conscious of the distinctions but were able to develop them in remarkable ways.

One brief example, from the essay by Marcel Mauss on 'La Prière et les Rites Oraux' (1909) will suffice. One method, he said, constitutes from the analysis of a number of phenomena a generic notion which can form the basis of comparative work (he cites the analysis of sacrifice undertaken by Hubert and himself as an example). A second method follows the phenomenon through a progressive series when it becomes more and more developed. This series is constituted 'outside of time and space' in a purely logical sequence. This analysis is called genetic (génétique), its first moment of explanation is the establishment of a genealogical classification (classification généalogique) of the phenomena in the order of their evolution. But in so arriving at a conception of lower and higher forms it is not intended to 'explain the complex by the simple' (Mauss, 1968–9: i, 394–7).

There are further aspects to the problem of causal complexity which appear in any examination of Durkheim's social analyses. One such example is Durkheim's own remarkable analogy of the complexity of social causality with that which might be active in adolescent sexual development. Strong impulses may well impel an adolescent towards what is culturally apprehended as an appropriate object, the opposite sex (say), but normal sexual desires only arise when relations with an individual of the opposite sex, who is also 'produced' as an appropriate object by the same fundamental causes, are entered into. It is the same, he says, of the structure of complex processes, the division of labour, for example, where 'two orders of fact meet, simply because they are the effects of the same cause' (Durkheim, 1964b: 274). With the advance of the division of labour, new phenomena can come into contact and be interconnected through 'mechanical adjustments' of their functioning. Thus the different effects of a single fundamental causal process become functionally interdependent (1964b: 275). This image of causal complexity avoids teleological psychological reasoning and recourse to providential harmonies. The effects themselves certainly carry tendencies and energies imparted from their cause, but no inherent inevitability of them finding their 'natural place' is invoked. The changing alignment of the functional equilibrium, and the contingent elements of the process of adjustment between effects and the effects with their causes (which have to be reproduced), open up the space for possible misalignments and deviations.

Let us examine some of these distinctions further. *Division*'s first chapter begins with a criticism of teleology and tries to present a workable conception of the relation between cause and function. Efficient cause in sociology is a cause which issues from the social itself: society is in this sense creative (there is also the proposition that indirect and conditional causation exists, particularly at the level of social morphology); function and functional interdependence is a second level logic which seems to involve some elements of teleology, specific to the phenomena of reproducing living systems. And every sociologist knows Durkheim's basic rule: the unique unity of one cause and one effect. Against Mill he argues that the same phenomenon cannot be the product of more than one cause or of different causes at different times. The relation is absolute and invariable. Complex phenomena exist of course. These are analysed by arguing that there are combinations of causes, the action of a number of different causes can converge in a single phenomenon. An example of this can be found in the approach to the study of suicide: 'if suicide depends on more than one cause it is because in reality there are several kinds of suicide' (Durkheim, 1982: 150).

There is a suggestion in the critical literature that Durkheim moved away from a conception of mechanical causation in the *Division* to more complex analyses after 1898. This is thrown into considerable doubt when it is clear that the same term was used in the essay 'Two Laws' of 1901 (Durkheim, 1978: 177). There was certainly a place for the action of mechanical, non-teleological causation in Durkheim's sociology, for the division of labour produced qualitatively new forms mechanically. There is also a hint of this in Durkheimian structuralism in 'Primitive Classification' (Durkheim and Mauss, 1963: 86). It is important to note some of Durkheim's own attempts to think out the problems on this point: in a footnote to the *Rules* he says

We were wrong to emphasise unduly physical density as being the exact expression of dynamic density. However, the substitution of the former for the latter is absolutely justified for everything relating to the economic effects of dynamic density, for instance the division of labour as a purely economic fact. (Durkheim, 1982: 146)

The point which seems significant here is that Durkheim established a base/superstructure conception of social forms, formulated in the early work in the opposition between material and moral density. In the *Division*, one expression of their relationship is agnostic: 'It is useless to try to find out which has determined the other: they are inseparable' (Durkheim, 1964b: 257); certainly this was modified but not completely rejected in the discussion in the *Rules,* as has been shown above.

One recent writer has exclaimed 'surely we must protest' and says: 'If either my wife or I get up to turn on the light, the effect in either case will be the same' (Schmaus, 1985: 19). Durkheim would have said that the cause in both cases was the same, for the produced distinction between efficient cause and human agency in precisely these examples is the whole basis of what Durkheim took to be the main thrust of scientific thought. It certainly does not diminish in Durkheim's work for the idea of such a univocal causation is to be found in *Elementary Forms* in the idea that religious phenomena can only have one basic cause, stated at the beginning of the work. It is not that this basic cause is simply a social cause but that it is a social cause of a certain type that remains in existence even in the advanced societies. The rationale for the study of elementary forms is that the gaps between cause and effect are not so wide as in the advanced societies, where analysis is complicated by the existence of derived phenomena. The idea of the separation between the cause and the effect is thus a key idea here:

> In proportion as it progresses in history, the causes which called it into existence, though remaining active, are no longer perceived except across a vast scheme of interpretations which quite transform them ... the psychological gap between the apparent cause and the effective cause, has become more considerable and more difficult for the mind to leap. (Durkheim, 1957: 20)

(v)

I want now to return to examine the problem of the concept of the social fact, and first to the controversy over whether Durkheim's discussion is even posed at a level of minimal logical acceptability.

The modern *locus classicus* of the view that Durkheim's work is seriously flawed because it contains unacceptable inconsistencies is the analysis made by Steven Lukes (1973: 12–15; Durkheim, 1982: 3–4). The charge is made specifically against definition the social fact, and

particularly its constraining character. Lukes identifies five illustrations of the definition: 1. legal and moral rules with sanctions;
2. requirement to follow rules or procedures in order to accomplish a
task; 3. influence of morphological factors; 4. compulsion of group
pressures; 5. socialisation and education or 'cultural determination'
(Lukes). Lukes suggests that:

> to call them all 'constraint' is, at the very least, confusing. One naturally
> understands 'constraint' in sense 1, that is, to refer to cases where an individual
> who wishes to act in one way is made to act in another: hence Durkheim's
> stress on the link between social constraint and 'the prestige with which
> certain representations are invested' and his talk of a 'power of coercion' by
> means of which 'ways of acting, thinking and feeling' are 'imposed' on the
> individual. Even here there would seem to be a distinction to be drawn (which
> Durkheim half sees) between cases of pure authority at one extreme (where
> compliance occurs because of the voluntary acceptance of legitimacy) and
> coercive power at the other (where it occurs because negative sanctions are
> feared). However, it seems clear that Durkheim's paradigm sense of 'con-
> straint' is the exercise of authority, backed by sanctions, to get individuals to
> conform to rules. It is obviously stretching the meaning of the word somewhat
> to apply it to sense 2 ... but to apply it to senses 3–5 is even more misleading,
> since these refer to what influences men's desires not to what thwarts them....'
> Lukes, 1973: 13)

This is probably a typical example of the level of Lukes' criticisms of
Durkheim throughout – detailed, but entirely unsympathetic to the
possibility of following an attempt to establish a definition which
slightly modifies an existing term, even though it is accompanied by
many examples and illustrations. The background of Lukes' criticism
is often inserted in such passages: Weber's concept of *verstehen* or, as
here, the concept of 'legitimacy' suitably humanised. The criticism if
analysed clause by clause is, however, surprisingly weak. Why should
there be an appeal to 'one naturally understands' by constraint the
thwarting of intention? It is more likely that Lukes is attempting to
smuggle in an assumption nowhere argued by him. It is perfectly
acceptable, even in English, to talk of the constraints imposed by
circumstances. It is also quite acceptable to talk of socialisation and
education as developing in the individual inner constraints, both intellectual and moral. Actually, the error here seems to be exposed in
Lukes' own next comment:

after the *Rules* [Durkheim] eventually ceased to stress the criterion of 'constraint'. He had intended it, he wrote, only as part of a preliminary, indicative definition of social facts: these latter, he admitted, can 'equally present the opposite characteristic' – that is, opposite to constraint in sense 1 – namely the attractive power of (internalised) ideals to which men are attached and which thereby influence their behaviour, the opposite pole of the moral life to 'duty' namely, 'the good'. (1973: 13–14)

Here Lukes has permitted Durkheim's project to emerge but only to commit a further misjudgment. It is quite untrue even to say that because Durkheim added to his sociology the analysis of the power of the 'good' that he 'ceased to stress' (Lukes) the power of 'duty'. It is also quite incorrect to suggest that he conceived the 'good' to be an aspect of moral authority that was different in principle. The difference is only an 'apparent contradiction' (Durkheim, 1982: 47); indeed they vary only in degree, for the 'mechanism of this phenomenon is the same' (Durkheim, 1953: 43).

Readings which emphasise the inconsistencies, ambiguities, of this text often resort to wrenching clauses out of sentences and sentences out of paragraphs in order to make their point, but with Lukes there is a direct failure even to follow, in what is an analysis in detail, the detailed steps of Durkheim's argument. If the first chapter of the *Rules* is read sentence by sentence, all Lukes' criticisms are answered, and from within the text itself. For example, Durkheim clearly distinguishes between moral facts and 'indirect' social facts, as Lukes himself acknowledges, (which is the crucial refocusing of formulation in the years 1893–4, as I have shown in an earlier chapter, which, if further misconceptions are not to arise must also be located in Durkheim's first outlines of his project in 1888, of the relation of moral facts in the category of social facts in general, a position recapitulated in 1906 (Durkheim, 1953: 71–2)). But in order to clarify just how these readings are carried out it is possible to demonstrate that, like these spurious readings which suggest Durkheim is either materialist or idealist, etc., there is simply a failure to grasp the project, or textual argument as a whole. On the one hand Durkheim talks of things (and has a theory of knowledge which places sensations in direct proximity to things) but he also talks of the immateriality of social objects (and a theory of knowledge which suggests that categories are socially produced); he suggests that morphological constraints exist (but are indirect), but also that motor constraints are, primarily, ideal and not physical; he suggests that classification in the first instance must be dominated by morphological considerations, yet it is moral density which is active (he was prepared to move to an aetiological classification in *Suicide* when he could not construct a morphological one); he suggests the uneven formula that moral ideals must be studied as things. Reductive readings can opt either for one of the poles (he is materialist or idealist), or that he is neither or both inconsistently; they seem fatally incapable of acknowledging the accessibility of the task Durkheim set himself.

(vi)
Finally I will examine, in relation to the question of the logical boundaries or limits of arguments, some of the criticisms of this work which suggest that it is empiricist. This charge comes from many different sources and each of the terms adopted have to be assessed themselves relative to the specific charge they make against Durkheim. This terminological Babel is not in itself unusual: but it is necessary here to ensure that the disputes are not pure logomachies. If no absolute definitions can be given or assumed, it is possible to identify whether terms are being used consistently and whether two writers are using the same term in the same way.

In the *Rules*, Durkheim seems to accept the dominant theory of knowledge in the empiricist tradition, even criticising Locke and Condillac for not being sufficiently radical in displacing prenotions (Durkheim, 1982: 71), but it is also maintained that the position of pure 'empiricism' is ultimately a mysticism, even the negation of all science (1982: 74). The position adopted is also distanced from positivism, which again is criticised for not displacing prenotions and elaborating a metaphysics (1982: 33); realism is also explicitly avoided through the recourse to the definition of the object of sociology as the social species, a concept which provides 'a middle ground between ... nominalism of the historians and the extreme realism of the philosophers' (1982: 108). A preface and a note, both added in 1895, indicated that the position is not materialist (1982: 32, 163) (while letters to Bouglé show that he wanted to distance himself from idealism (Besnard, 1983: 53)).

Critics must adopt a view which can only imply that Durkheim's own claims are utterly confused, that he wrongly classifies and describes his own practice, or that he is working with a different set of conceptions from those used in philosophical traditions current in Durkheim's times. Each of these have been suggested at various times. All that Durkheim was prepared to say was a) that his position was objective, scientific and rationalist in the sense that he believed that social facts were knowable through the application of scientific method, i.e., to treat the object as natural and external to the mind of the observer, and b) that the object, 'the social fact' was an 'immateriality *sui generis*' (1982: 162). If there are rationalist appeals to the sociologist to 'throw off the yoke of empirical categories', just as there are assumptions to the effect that the object to be analysed is external to the observer, and cannot, therefore be reached by introspection, it must also be remembered that the *Rules* also holds that the only way contact can be made with things is through an initial empirical work on representations via an objective index of them.

If we return directly to the criticism that Durkheim is 'crudely empiricist' and take an example we find even a commonly accepted analysis rests on a very questionable reading of Durkheim. Bryant, for example, follows others (see Hirst, 1975: 109) in arguing that it was pure 'nonsense' when Durkheim suggested that physics tried to measure heat more adequately by developing the thermometer and that the concept of heat was produced out of these improved sense impressions (Bryant, 1985: 37). But did Durkheim propose this 'nonsense'? All he says is that the sociologist must try to follow the physicist in trying to substitute 'vague impressions' by introducing more reliable instruments (Durkheim, 1982: 81), as in the *Division* he said science studies 'heat through the variations in volume which changes in temperature produce in bodies' (Durkheim, 1964a: 66), concluding that sociology should adopt the same capacity in its own field. Later in the *Rules* Durkheim explicitly refers to the 'strange ratiocinations that the doctors of the Middle Ages constructed from their notions of heat and cold', which were 'confused notions' (Durkheim, 1982: 66), yet not without a basis in reality. When Bryant quotes Durkheim to the effect that 'it is from observable data that [science] should derive directly the elements for its initial definition' (Durkheim, 1982: 81), it is to suggest directly that the movement from the sensation to the concept is unproblematic and continuous.

The problem is this. There is no doubt that at certain points Durkheim uses a language which can be read in this way – words express things, science must begin by creating words which express the nature of the thing as it is experienced in immediate sensations, indeed it must take, derive, borrow elements from the *données sensibles*, the direct link between the external thing and the initial representation to form the initial definition itself. Bryant's argument is that no such sensation can figure in a definition, therefore Durkheim's argument is nonsense. Hirst's formulation is that 'neither deduction nor principles are matters of sensation nor are they given in nature, unless, of course, nature *thinks*' (Hirst, 1975: 107). But the question is not so simple (unless one thinks human action is not part of nature) since Durkheim is not saying that concepts are only a matter of human sensation, but that science has as its raw materials elements which are not purely ideational and, further, it is to such raw materials that the sociologist should find the point of departure of all concepts.

The real complication is not perhaps that this is crude empiricism – for it is an emphasis on the empirical combined with an attack on 'empiricism' – but it is inconsistent with the idea that knowledge is socially produced, the charge made by Marshall Sahlins (i.e., that this thesis of Durkheim's is contradicted by the proposition that general ideas come to the individual through education, etc.). There can be little doubt that there is a serious tension here, but it is only an inconsistency if other conditions are present, (e.g. Lukes is certainly in error again to think that only the cultural facts of previous generations (passed down from generation to generation) should be thought external to individuals in society). For Durkheim the collectivity is creative of representations, and these are formed, logically, outside the individual.

But this only brings us back to the beginning of the circle of Durkheimian sociology.

16

Conclusions

I have attempted to show that Durkheim's classic essay the *Rules* is a more serious work than is generally recognised, is not based on simplistic principles, and, far from constituting a methodological summa was, for the Durkheimians, a treasure house of ideas and methodological suggestions. Sociologists have in general failed to meet the challenge of this work and have treated it, not as a brilliantly inventive work of popularisation, but as pseudo-scientific dogmatism. If sociologists have found it full of inconsistencies, and hold that it was never applied even by Durkheim in his sociological investigations (somewhat misleading, as we have seen) their denunciations have a persistence and variety that suggest they have never really seemed to have got to the bottom of its mysteries, for they have been recommenced at regular intervals. This is almost certainly because, despite being written clearly and vigorously, it is part of a sociological and philosophical tradition of great sophistication and considerable achievement. Even those who have criticised Durkheim's theory as seriously flawed have had to admit, 'whatever its shortcomings, Durkheimian dogma has proved a remarkably productive and progressive research programme.' (Lukes, in his introduction to the *Rules* (Durkheim, 1982: 18).)

I have shown how the commentators have refused to follow Durkheim's way of linking methodological elements in a complex strategic path through the thickets of fixed polarised oppositions that dogged philosophical and social research, and that his work has been seen as either paradoxical, or eclectic. And, because insufficient care has been taken to consider the framework of his development, spurious efforts which tried to identify vast changes of theory have been common. In order to avoid these mistakes it has been necessary to reconstruct the unifying threads of this work, and in so doing it has become clear that this unity is fundamentally connected to the ultimate aim and motivating force of the enterprise, the continuation of the radical Enlightenment enterprise which had 'miscarried' in the Revolutions of 1789, 1848, and 1871, through failures to understand the true complexity of social transformations. But today there are possibilities for the emergence of a new and more adequate assessment of Durkheim's project, and here a new assessment of the *Rules* will play a key part.

(i)

The brilliant character of the *Rules* is well known. As a manifesto it is bristling with ideas, with illustrations, criticisms, with ingenious manoeuvres. Its argument is, at one level, very simple: these are the problems it proclaims, and these are the means for dealing with them. Of course the very title of the work has, as Bernard Lacroix has noted (Lacroix, 1979: 88) implicit references to Descartes' *Discourse on Method* and *Rules for the Direction of the Mind,* but he was wrong to suggest that it is only at the beginning of the *Rules* that Durkheim evokes the function of the I (in 'when I fulfil my obligations', etc.,) for Durkheim uses this technique in many of his inventories (see Durkheim, 1953: 80; 1961: 489; 1964b: 420; etc.) it even reappears in the *Rules* (Durkheim, 1982: 130). At the very general level of the organisation of the book, the reader moves from a conspectus of the kinds of topics there are available for sociology to the discipline of 'observing' them, and their classification into normal and pathological types, in order to facilitate practice, is dependent on being able to identify normal societal types. Rules for sociological explanation, verification and the demonstration of proofs are all similarly connected and are dependent on the theory of the normal motivating social forces. The formal unity of the book and its related forms of expositionary logic are therefore strikingly interdependent, a characteristic which has failed to attract the analysis it deserves (though it was noticed at an early date (e.g. Deploige)).

There is one major problem, however, with this logical circle, and it is a weakness around which has grown a whole tradition of misunderstanding: by beginning with the definition of the social fact and suggesting that it is within the register of the social fact that sociologists must find their topics for investigation, the argument has been disconnected from Durkheim's own problems in a way which departs seriously from his initial discussion of these issues in his lectures and writings of 1888 and 1893. There, it was the sociological problem which was posed as the real starting point: the attempt to define the terrain of relevant social facts was begun as an auxiliary requirement of the way the problem had been posed (Durkheim, 1964b: 424; 1978: 214): e.g. how is it possible to recognise a custom, or a moral fact? But even there the underlying political objectives of Durkheim's project were not identified as motivating the research; these objectives, though stated in reviews and other writings, were based on an already elaborate diagnosis of the form of the crisis through which modern France was passing and, indeed, he had already specified the nature of the remedy called for. If this perspective on Durkheim's work is pursued, as it is by many critics, his recourse to scientific and strategic analysis could be seen (ungenerously (Hirst, Benton, Marshall, etc.) as an elaborate mystification, or (more generously) as an attempt to present the most rigorous case, while still engaged in these crucial social struggles. While Durkheim's consistent loyalty to the view that modern societies suffered from a chronic lack of institutional solidarity cannot be denied, one of the important aspects of the assessment of his work is to judge it relative to this objective: in other words, to examine the extent to which his projects actually deepened an understanding of this problem, or the extent to which the initial ideas intervened to prevent an analysis of them. Whatever the outcome of these investigations, as far as the *Rules* is concerned, Durkheim only very rarely allowed them to surface directly and explicitly as such, yet without them the work would appear merely to make the claim that sociology had a right to exist as an academic discipline, and further, that it should become the preeminent and dominant social discipline. It would be for others to make something of its fruits.

(ii)

In sum, the basic ideas of the book are organised around two main thematic threads: the attempt to define the content of sociology, and the attempt to define appropriate methodological procedures.

Although the work begins with an examination of the social fact, the real problem is that both it and the classification of normal and abnormal facts are subordinate to the identification of the normal societal type or species. The political project rests on the ability of the sociologist to be able to distinguish between normal and abnormal social facts (significantly Durkheim shows that even applying elementary rational rules some utopian theses concerning what is abnormal must be rejected). The order of discussion thus gravitates towards social classification, yet how societies are to be classified partly depends on the level of elaboration of the theory of the nature of societies, for Durkheim wanted to develop not a descriptive account but a causal theory. Discussion of this is further delayed but it emerges eventually in his discussion of sociological explanation, for it is here that the question of what is primary and what secondary in the make up of social formations is approached as a theoretical issue.

Rules for the identification of the social fact, for observing it, for classifying it and explaining it also have a centre of gravity. All the problems of epistemology and philosophy also revolve around it: Durkheim's adherence to the view that the methodological goal of sociology is to engage in the work of constructing genuinely objective experiments. It governs the theory of knowledge, the articulation of both empirical and categorial registers. Durkheim's aim is to create crucial and decisive experiments that will produce laws which will be true for all countries and all time, since these will remove controversy surrounding the diagnosis of the dominant social ills. But the constitution of meaningful experiments in sociology is fraught with difficulties: they have to be indirect (the materials cannot be manipulated), they cannot be successful simply by comparing immediately given elements.

Durkheim is forced, however, in the *Rules* to identify alternative procedures, for in some cases the availability of even a small number of relevant facts is in doubt, or facts may not be available in the right form to enable experimentation to occur. His preferred method is to work on external objective characteristics of facts, produced in the right way, which have been rationally ordered and, by applying the comparative method, to work towards an understanding of inner connections. But his basic problem, the identification of the form of crisis in modern France, could not be approached through this method. In the case of his analysis of suicide rates, which certainly aimed to establish that the rate in France was abnormal, he could not even establish a classification using external characteristics at all. He found an ingenious solution (and one perhaps suggested even in the *Rules*) to this problem. But there was another, and that was how to establish, if the suicide rates could be shown as possibly indicating an abnormal condition, the specific social causes of such abnormalities. The main danger in these procedures, he argued in the *Rules*, was that the force of intuition and wishful thinking is not sufficiently checked and counterbalanced. We might add that the possibly pseudo-scientific conclusions would also have the dubious legitimacy of being produced by the 'objective method', and this could have the counterproductive consequence of bringing the whole attempt into disrepute. Visible here is the classic opposition of desire and fact, which the whole of the methodological venture was designed to cope with. The danger lies in a victory of desire over the necessary discipline (constraints) in which the outcome is an analysis which is expressed in the form of 'it is so' when all that can be said is 'it would suit if it were so' (see Needham, in Durkheim and Mauss, 1963, xxi); it is in fact nothing but the subjective method in the guise of the objective method.

(iii)

The least understood aspect of Durkheim's position (partly because it is pushed to one side in the *Rules*) is the way in which the sociological project itself is socially and historically situated. At the back of Durkheim's theory there is an elaborate sociology of sociology: it constitutes a remarkable circle, for as society itself develops, even into crises, so the categories it generates are reproduced in its forms of knowledge. Sociology itself is socially caused and has the character, as it develops into an academic discipline, of a social fact. This is why the *Rules* is presented as part of a sociological tradition, an intellectual movement. The text of the *Rules* indicates that a significant reeducation is necessary for the sociologist, who must learn to think in a new way, an effort implied by the very nature of the advanced societies. But Durkheim's construction of the conditions of the emergence of sociology, as we have examined it in the previous chapter, acknowledges many heterogeneous contributing forces.

The idea that social movements or institutions are built up by accretion was one of Durkheim's earliest themes: the idea, for example, that the modern family 'contains within itself ... the entire historical development of the family' ((1888), Durkheim, 1978: 211); cross-historical comparison was one way of experimenting with elements to find a more abstract and general level of truth. Thus it was in a sense natural to return to the simplest forms and so to anthropological study, but always to return to a better understanding of the present and the question of normal forms of solidarity.

If Durkheim's effort was not, even in the study of history and anthropology, a simple academic 'archaeology' (Durkheim, 1977: 14), but aimed to return to instruct the present, to whom was the sociology addressed? The renaissance intellectual submitted his work to a prince (Gramsci to a modern prince). Durkheim's work, with all its energies devoted to diagnosis, was without its prince: it was apparently to remain divorced from the impurities of political prejudices and party struggles. Indeed, he thought the qualities demanded of academics and politicians were so radically different that to become a politician would virtually mean to cease to be an intellectual (Durkheim, 1972). A talent in one direction (abstract thought) would not be complemented in the other ('practical grasp'). This attempt to remain both divorced from, even 'above' social struggles, while producing social analysis which had as its aim practical results, was associated, not with a failure to develop a political theory, but with a failure to connect the specific nature of what he proposed with the conditions for the possibility of its being done. In the outcome, his theories were in fact adopted in a form by Italian fascists in the 1920s, and even Mauss a decade later sought to rectify what he imagined was Durkheim's element of responsibility for totalitarianism (see Gane, 1984), a common theme in the 1930s (see the Introduction to the first translation of the *Rules*). This is difficult to imagine now that the modern emphasis has been firmly placed on Durkheim's supposedly liberal-conservative disposition. The general weakness in Durkheim's practice, the absence of a concrete connection between his theoretical diagnosis and the implementation of the remedy, seems to stem from the belief that the crucial determinants of social development lie behind actual political struggle, within public opinion – which is the ultimate arbiter and perhaps Durkheim's own modern prince.

This weakness may also be linked to another principal emphasis of Durkheim's work: the very search for incontrovertible truth (through the application of the objective method) downgraded the significance of political debate. It is possible to identify a violent tension in Durkheim here, between the acknowledgment of the importance of strategic struggle in complex transitions (especially developed in his work on educational change), with elements, noticeable in the *Rules* at famous and well known junctures in the argument, which emphasise the clearing away of 'prenotions', the systematic removal of the *idola* of everyday life. Elsewhere, in a similar vein, the sociologist is encouraged to make a *tabula rasa* of his preconceptions before engaging in analysis (Durkheim, 1978: 86). All this bears a striking resemblance to what he says political extremists attempt to do:

> Almost all say there is complete incompatibility between what ought to be and what is, and that the existing order must disappear to give place to a new. In this sense they are revolutionary ... [and] this subversive spirit comes from ... the integral character their demands assume. (1962: 171)

This problem is acute in the *Rules* which can now be seen in Durkheim's own terms as a revolutionary manifesto (at least in its dominant themes). And it is precisely here, if we follow Durkheim's own critique of this position, that problems arise, for it is at this point – the struggle against prenotions – that the social struggle is at stake: but this approach suppresses the processes of social dialectic, deflects the question of the social struggle for a remedy of social disease, and is associated with an incipient elitism in an attempt to create an esoteric discipline.

(iv)

We can now return to examine the strategic weaknesses of Durkheim's sociology, for if we take the point of view that the main sociological investigations were designed to open the question of the need for greater institutional solidarity, it is clear that there are grave problems in the specific ways in which Durkheim aligned his projects. The *Division*, for example, in approaching the analysis of abnormal forms of the division of labour, could not employ the method advocated (through 'the average case') and could only do so by analogy with a previous state (Durkheim, 1964b: 435, 370) or by structural analysis (Durkheim, 1982: 97, 95). The previous state, however, was of course the condition of medieval guild society. In other words, the elaborate apparatus of the rules had produced the argument that the restoration of something 'functionally equivalent' to the guilds, i.e., socialism, was required because modern society was of the same species as medieval society. No wonder Durkheim advised against the use of this method, for how could it be anything but a minimal check against the desired solution when not only was there a question of functional comparison and structural analysis (brilliant suggestions in themselves) but also the intervention of the biological analogy to support the idea that medieval and modern societies were of the same species. Without further methodological constraints the outcome was virtually a foregone conclusion.

The strategic significance of *Elementary Forms* is even more remote.

By examining the cluster of elements around Aboriginal totemism it was hoped to show essential components of all societies, since the processes of social production and renewal were caused by social energies which have universal features: these are particularly transparent in less complicated structures. Thus, tacked on to the end of the analysis of totemism, is a brief coda which traces the evolution of religion, the formation of science, and ends by predicting a new cultural effervescence which will be the structural equivalent of the Aboriginal corrobbori, but transformed to meet the needs of the languishing advanced society.

But the problem of the analysis of *Suicide* is in a sense equally difficult, for here Durkheim tried to show that the modern crisis had produced abnormally high suicide rates. The choice of suicide rates themselves, just like totemism as the archetypal elementary religious form, was immediately criticised as ill-advised. Suicide rates were notoriously unreliable, as Mauss quickly acknowledged, the variations which Durkheim wanted to establish were extremely marginal (with such very small rates), but above all the attempt to work from an external index towards the inner connections was impossible to accomplish since, according to Durkheim, there were complicated mixed types of suicide as well as no obvious correlation between the way the suicide was accomplished and its social causes. Ingeniously, Durkheim 'reversed' the order of analysis, and established a 'morphological classification' from an aetiological one. Even so, it was immediately pointed out (Durkheim, 1964b: 19), the remedy for such abnormalities of suicide rates as could be determined in this 'devious' analysis, the restoration of the guilds, 'was not proportional to the extent of the evil'.

The question is not so easily decided in the case of *Educational Thought,* for the objective was not to reach a way of finding a judgment on the guilds, but one on the nature and content of modern education. The objective of a recourse in this case to history was ultimately practical: but what was the kind of history undertaken? Some writers (e.g. Lukes) have thought that the methods of this style of work had no precursors before 1895:

> In the *Rules* he assigned it a very minor place, a mere adjunct.... But after the watershed of 1895, he came to see it as offering the possibility of a crucial laboratory test for his general sociological theories. (Lukes in Durkheim, 1982: 10)

This view is entirely mistaken, as any reference to Durkheim's early writings on method will show (Durkheim, 1978:211). But there is a problem in how to reconcile Durkheim's views on the comparative method and historical analysis. In fact this is not at all difficult, for Durkheim's conception of this kind of history is already at considerable distance from simple descriptive history. Indeed, looked at as 'comparative history' rather than simple narration Durkheim even went to identify it with a fundamental aspect of sociological method itself (note the characteristic caveat):

the principal problems of sociology consist in researching the way in which ... [an] institution ... was established, what causes gave rise to it, and to what useful ends it responds. Comparative history, understood in the sense which we are going to try to specify, is the only instrument of the sociologist disposed to resolve these kinds of questions. ((1909), Durkheim, 1978:83)

If Durkheim had stopped there it would still be possible to reconcile evolutionary analysis and comparative historical analysis; but it is clear that the argument continues, since the objective of sociological analysis is not simply to undertake historical comparisons, but to 'extend' history 'in a certain way'; it is to experiment:

[which] consists in making a fact vary, of producing it in various forms which are subsequently methodically compared. The sociologist cannot therefore limit himself to the consideration of a single people or even of a single era. He must compare societies of the same type and also of different types. ... The comparative method is thus the preeminent instrument. (1978:85)

If we follow up this distinction it is clear why Durkheim entitled his lecture course a 'history' and not as the posthumously published title has it an 'evolution', a term which Durkheim generally reserved for more abstract comparative constructions. This might be understood as follows: there are two levels of analysis, those concerning concrete existing societies in time and space (an historical sequence, or it could be a single synchronic system with analysis focussing on internal comparisons, as was attempted in parts of the project on suicide rates, and in the *Elementary Forms*), and more abstract comparisons (what was called 'genetic' analysis, i.e., an evolutionary sequence of materials from different societies, or a 'generic' analysis which combined such materials into a composite picture (on this see Hubert and Mauss (1899), 1964)) projected onto a plane outside of time and place. It is on this latter, uchronic plane that Durkheim demands that the comparisons take account of the relative stage of development of institutions or societies (isochronic comparison), as well as across levels of complexity (genealogical, or diachronic comparison). But again what distinguishes this approach is its adherence to the principles of the key to Durkheim's method: the indirect experiment.

This clarifies the project in *Educational Thought* considerably, and clears up the confusions concerning falsely invoked discontinuities in Durkheim's thought. The analysis is a certain kind of comparative history: it attempts to follow the ways in which, from an original complex nucleus, an institution grows through progressive accumulation and reorganisation. The contemporary institution may appear simple enough, but historical analysis reveals by comparisons that it is made up of diverse elements. Thus constant movement between the past and the present reveals unexpected elements in the present. But historical analysis also reveals elements available in past practice which, though valuable, even essential, have been unnecessarily discarded, creating continuous problems in the present:

> The Renaissance succeeds Scholasticism: the men of the Renaissance immediately took it as self-evident that there was nothing worth preserving in the system of the Scholastics. We shall have to ask whether this revolutionary approach did not produce certain gaps in our educational ideal. (Durkheim, 1977: 17, trans mod)

Thus Durkheim's history is also evaluative: as it analyses it also compares the elements of the practice of each epoch with a view to restoring, where necessary, the best for a more adequate present practice. The modern revolution should in part be a renaissance. But where it might be expected that his conclusion would be for modern education to be centred on sociological teaching (since virtually all interpreters see him as an obsessive academic imperialist) he actually said: 'given the rudimentary state in which (the social sciences) are at present they are in no position to serve our purposes. ...' He again refers to 'the few abstract, fragmentary and disputable propositions which the cultural sciences have succeeded in setting forth' (1977: 331). And concludes that the curriculum must be a balance of historical, linguistic and scientific cultures.

But what is of immediate interest here is the link between Durkheim's survey of French educational ideals and the project in the *Rules*, for what is surprising is that the links and parallels between the two are hardly superficial: the project encapsulates all the principal sources later identified by Durkheim in *Educational Thought*, with the one very important different emphasis at one point, as I have already noted. For Durkheim continues the tradition of rationalist faith in reason and emphasis on clarity (Cartesianism, and Jesuit training), Enlightenment doctrines of complex objects and the materialist theory of knowledge that the source of all knowledge lies in sensation (Condorcet), together with the critique of empiricism in Aristoteleanism (1977: 151) also mentioned in his essay on Montesquieu ('observation is suspect until it is confirmed by reason' (Durkheim, 1965: 55)). The major addition to these elements of educational theory of the Revolutionary epoch (Durkheim, 1977: 298), and taken up again in Durkheim's period, was the application of experimental reason to the study of the social world (but without as yet sufficient results to form the basis of general education).

What Durkheim attempts to do in the *Rules*, therefore, may be considered as a strategic accumulation, a parallel to the ways in which institutions progress through historical accumulation; just as history naturally seems to combine elements into organised wholes (1977: 15), so Durkheim has replicated in his own way this complexity by attempting to restore the most important contributions from the past whilst still recognising their heterogeneous origins. The conclusions and recommendations of *Educational Thought* point in the direction of a critical historical synthesis; it seems possible to reflect that this is precisely the internal heterogeneous structure of the *Rules*.

(v)

Durkheim's theses on the formation of sociology, however, went further in two senses at least, as we noted earlier; first, at the end of his lectures (1896) on socialism, he suggested that the progress of sociology seemed to be bound to parallel movements of religion and socialism (in itself an interesting application of the sociological method). They were found 'connected' together in the work of Saint-Simon, and they seemed to flourish or decline together historically. Although they appeared, from one point of view, antagonistic to one another, Durkheim suggested that this was because each 'expresses only one aspect of social reality' so that if practice is to be advanced it was necessary to 'habitually take account of their different tendencies and discover their unity' (Durkheim, 1962: 284–5). And, secondly, within the development of sociology itself there were also different tendencies. He identified two currents: one dominated by Marxist conceptions, which followed a naive evolutionism and sought to relate analysis (a reductionist one according to Durkheim) to the problem of a return to a simple society (Letourneau); and another which tended to reduce social to individual phenomena (Tarde); both of these were hostile to his own complex sociology (1975a: i, 73–108).

Together with these views Durkheim developed the thesis that conditions in other countries were, in general, far less conducive to the development of sociology; not only did France have the greatest need ('there is no country where the old organisation has been uprooted more completely and where consequently . . . there is greater need for . . . science'), but it also had the greatest faith in rationalism; sociology would succeed if rationalism could be transformed (1960a: 383–4). In other countries, attempts to develop sociology either floundered on individualism and empiricism (Anglo-Saxon cultures) or on philosophical metaphysics (Germanic cultures), the two principal obstacles to the attempt to develop social sciences.

(vi)

All of these efforts at situating the sociological project, of identifying the preconditions for its development, of specifying the kind of education that might serve as preparation for its practice, were all explicitly discussed in the *Rules*, for sociology needs not only a method but also practitioners, who had to be formed. The *Rules* was, then, also an educational document, and as such a part of its success has no doubt come from its revolutionary ardour. But how are we to assess its key lines of argument today? Surprisingly, against the judgments of writers like Pickering, cited earlier, Durkheim's conception of science is remarkably in line with the main trends of modern, particularly French, philosophy of science, as Lacroix has pointed out (1979). Certainly, the idea that each science has an epistemological structure that is unique to it is supported in the work of Bachelard, Koyre, Canguilhem, and others. Foucault's celebrated methodological fertility again seems to owe a great, largely unacknowledged, debt to Durkheim's suggestions, especially its development of the genealogical method, and, parallel with Canguilhem's investigations, has developed a critical analysis of the problematic distinction between the normal and the pathological.

While it is clear where the main lines of Durkheim's influence have been in Anglo-Saxon social sciences (for whatever Marshall (1974–5) may have said about Durkheim's disastrous effect on anthropology, it has been anthropology above all perhaps which has been the most successful discipline in the social sciences), this is not so in France, where Durkheim's considerable influence seems heavily disguised and indirect. For all that, a recent study of the work of Merleau-Ponty by James Schmidt cited a remark by Bourdieu and Passeron (1967) to the effect that: 'all the social sciences now live in the house of Durkheimianism, unbeknownst to them, as it were, because they walked into it backwards'; and Schmidt adds:

it would not be surprising if, sneaking out of Durkheim's house in the dead of night, they should run into a familiar figure, slipping out of Descartes's house. Meeting in that no-man's land where for better or for worse, the human sciences seem condemned to camp out for the foreseeable future, they might greet each other with a smile of recognition. (Schmidt, 1985: 165–6)

The problem is: who is right, Bourdieu and Passeron, or Schmidt? My hunch is that as far as the social sciences are concerned, and sociology in particular, they may be occupying the rooms of the house one of the cellars of which was constructed by Durkheim, but his spirit roams freely throughout.

Bibliography

I have not sought to burden the text with a substantial set of references. These have been kept to a minimum, and the Bibliography contains only titles of those works cited. For readers who would like further references these can be obtained via Lukes (1973: 561–615), and two bibliographies in *Revue Française de Sociologie*: 1976, Vol. 17 (343–53), and 1979, Vol. 20 (293–9). For references after 1979 the reader is referred to the specialist bulletin, *Etudes Durkheimiennes* (especially nos: 1; 2; 4; 5; 7; 9; 10), published by the Groupe d'études Durkheimiennes at the Fondation Maison des Sciences de l'Homme, 54, Boulevard Raspail, 75270 Paris, France.

Aimard, G. 1962. *Durkheim et la Science Economique*, Paris, Presses Universitaires de France

Alexander, G. 1982. *Theoretical Logic in Sociology, The Antinomies of Classical Thought: Marx and Durkheim*, vol. 2, London, Routledge & Kegan Paul

Alpert, H. 1939. *Emile Durkheim and His Sociology*, New York, Columbia University Press

Althusser, L. and Balibar, E. 1970. *Reading Capital*, London, New Left Books

Barnes, H. E. 1920. Durkheim's contribution to the reconstruction of political theory. In *Political Science Quarterly*, 35, 236–54

Benton, T. 1977. *Philosophical Foundations of the Three Sociologies*, London, Routledge & Kegan Paul

Besnard, P. (ed.) 1983. *The Sociological Domain*, Cambridge, Cambridge University Press

1984. L'anomie dans la biographie intellectuelle de Durkheim. In *Sociologie et Sociétés*, xiv. 2, 45–53

Bourdieu, P. and Passeron, J.-C., 1967. Sociology and Philosophy in France since 1945. *Social Research*, 34, 162–212

Bryant, C. 1985. *Positivism in Sociological Theory and Research*, Basingstoke, Macmillan

Clark, T. N. 1973. *Prophets and Patrons: The French University and the Emergence of the Social Sciences*, Cambridge Mass., Harvard University Press

Deploige, S. 1938 (1911). *The Conflict Between Ethics and Sociology*, St. Louis, Herder

Durkheim, E. 1915. *Germany Above All*, Paris, Colin

    1953. *Sociology and Philosophy*, London, Cohen and West

    1957. *Professional Ethics and Civic Morals*, London, Routledge & Kegan Paul

    1960a. *Essays on Sociology and Philosophy by Emile Durkheim et al.*, (ed.) K. H. Wolff, New York, Harper and Row

    1960b. *Socialism*, New York, Collier

    1961. *The Elementary Forms of the Religious Life*, New York, Collier-Macmillan

    1962. *Socialism*, New York, Collier-Macmillan

    1964a. *The Rules of Sociological Method*, New York, Free Press

    1964b. *The Division of Labour in Society*, London, Collier-Macmillan

    1965. *Montesquieu and Rousseau*, Ann Arbor, University of Michigan Press

    1970. *Suicide*, London, Routledge & Kegan Paul

    1973a. *Emile Durkheim on Morality and Society*, (ed.) R. N. Bellah, Chicago, University of Chicago Press

    1973b. *Moral Education*, New York, Free Press

    1975a. *Textes*, 3 vols, (ed.) V. Karady, Paris, Minuit

    1975b. *Durkheim on Religion*, (ed.) W. S. F. Pickering, London, Routledge & Kegan Paul

    1976. The role of the universities in the social education of the country. In *Minerva* 14, 380–8

    1977. *The Evolution of Educational Thought in France*, London, Routledge & Kegan Paul

    1978. *Emile Durkheim on Institutional Analysis*, (ed.) M. Traugott, Chicago, University of Chicago Press

    1980. *Emile Durkheim: Contributions to l'Année Sociologique*, (ed.) Y. Nandan, New York, Free Press

    1982. *The Rules of Sociological Method*, Basingstoke, Macmillan

    1983. *Pragmatism and Sociology*, Cambridge, Cambridge University Press

    1984. *The Division of Labour in Society*, Basingstoke, Macmillan

    1986. *Durkheim on Politics and the State*, Oxford, Polity Press

Durkheim, E. and Mauss, M. 1963. *Primitive Classification*, London, Cohen and West

Fauconnet, P. and Mauss, M. 1901. Sociologie. In Mauss, M., *Oeuvres*, vol. 3

Fenton, S. 1984. *Durkheim and Modern Sociology*, Cambridge, Cambridge University Press

Filloux, J. C. 1977. *Durkheim et le Socialisme*, Geneva, Droz

Filmer, P. *et al.*, 1972. *New Directions in Sociological Theory*, London, Collier-Macmillan

Fletcher, R. 1971. *The Making of Modern Sociology*, 2 vols, London, Nelson

Galton, F. *et al.* 1905. *Sociological Papers*, London, Macmillan

Gane, M. 1983a. Durkheim: the sacred language. In *Economy and Society*, 12, 1–47

   1983b. Durkheim: woman as outsider. In *Economy and Society*, 12, 227–70

   1984. Institutional socialism and the sociological critique of communism. In *Economy and Society*, 13, 305–30

Gehlke, C. E. 1915. *Emile Durkheim's Contributions to Sociological Theory*, New York, Columbia University Press

Giddens, A. 1971. *Capitalism and Modern Social Theory*, Cambridge, Cambridge University Press

   1972. *Emile Durkheim: Selected Writings*, Cambridge, Cambridge University Press

   1976. *New Rules of Sociological Method*, London, Hutchinson

   1977. *Studies in Social and Political Theory*, London, Hutchinson

   1978. *Durkheim*, Glasgow, Fontana

Gieryn, T. F. 1982. Durkheim's sociology of scientific knowledge. In *Journal of the History of the Behavioural Sciences*, 18, 107–29

Gisbert, P. 1959. Social facts and Durkheim's system. In *Anthropos*, 54, 353–69

Goffman, E. 1981. *Forms of Talk*, Oxford, Blackwell

Gurvitch, G. 1950. *La Vocation Actuelle de la Sociologie*, Paris, PUF

Haralambos, M. 1980. *Sociology, Themes and Perspectives*, Slough, University Tutorial Press

Hirst, P. 1975. *Durkheim, Bernard and Epistemology*, London, Routledge & Kegan Paul

Hubert and Mauss, M. 1964. *Sacrifice: Its Nature and Function*, London, Routledge & Kegan Paul

Johnson, T., Dandeker, A., and Ashworth, C. 1984. *The Structure of Social Theory*, Basingstoke, Macmillan

Jones, R. A. 1986. *Emile Durkheim*, London, Sage

Keat, R. and Urry, J. 1984. *Social Theory as Science*, London, Routledge & Kegan Paul

LaCapra, D. 1972. *Emile Durkheim: Sociologist and Philosopher*, Ithaca, Cornell University Press

Lacombe, R. 1926. *La Méthode Sociologique de Durkheim*, Paris, Alcan

Lacroix, B. 1979. The Elementary Forms as a reflection on power. In *Critique of Anthropology*, nos. 13–14, 87–104

1981. *Durkheim et la Politique*, Paris, Presses de la Fondation Nationale des Sciences Politiques

Lee, D. and Newby, H. 1983. *The Problem of Sociology*, London, Hutchinson

Lévi-Strauss, C. 1945. French Sociology. In Gurvitch, G. and Moore, W. E. (eds) *Twentieth Century Sociology*, New York, Philosophical Library

1972. *Structural Anthropology*, Vol. 1, Harmondsworth, Penguin

Lukes, S. 1973. *Emile Durkheim*, London, Allen Lane

Marshall, G. 1974–5, Durkheim and British Social Anthropology. In *Sociological Theory and Analysis*, iv, 3–46; v, 3–52

Mauss, M. 1968–9. *Oeuvres*, 3 Vols, Paris, Minuit

Monnerot, J. 1946. *Les Faits Sociaux ne sont pas des Choses*, Paris, Gallimard

Nisbet, R. A. 1965. *Emile Durkheim*, Englewood Cliffs, New Jersey, Prentice-Hall

1974. *The Sociology of Emile Durkheim*, New York, Oxford University Press

Parsons, T. 1937. *The Structure of Social Action*, Chicago, Free Press

Pickering, W. S. F. 1984. *Durkheim's Sociology of Religion*, London, Routledge & Kegan Paul

Pope, W., Cohen, J., and Hazelrigg, L. 1975. On the divergence of Weber and Durkheim: a critique of Parsons' convergence thesis. In *American Sociological Review*, 40, 4, 417–27

Pope, W. and Johnson, B. 1983. Inside Organic Solidarity. In *American Sociological Review*, 48, 681–92

Radcliffe-Brown, R. A. 1913. Three tribes of Western Australia. In *Journal of the Royal Anthropological Institute*, xliii, 143–94

Rex, J. 1961. *Key Problems in Social Theory*, London, Routledge & Kegan Paul

Ricoeur, P. 1949. *Philosophie de la Volonté*, Vol. 1, Paris, Aubier

Roche, M. 1976. A Durkheim reader. In *Writing Sociology*, 1, 9–23

Sahlins, M. 1976. *Culture and Practical Reason*, Chicago, University of Chicago Press

Schmaus, W. 1985. Hypotheses and historical analysis in Durkheim's sociological methodology: A Comtean tradition. In *Studies in History and Philosophy of Science*, 16, 1–30

Schmidt, J. 1985. *Maurice Merleau-Ponty*, Basingstoke, Macmillan

Seignobos, C. 1901. *La Méthode Historique*, Paris, Alcan

Smart, B. 1976. *Sociology, Phenomenology and Marxian Analysis*, London, Routledge & Kegan Paul

Sorel, A. 1895. Les Théories de M. Durkheim. In *Le Devenir Social*, 1, 1–26; 148–80

  1961. *Reflections on Violence*, New York, Collier

Tarde, G. 1899. *Social Laws*, New York, Macmillan

  1903. *The Laws of Imitation*, New York, Holt

  1969. *Gabriel Tarde: On Communication and Social Influence*, Chicago, Chicago University Press

Tosti, G. 1898. The delusions of Durkheim's sociological objectivism. In *American Journal of Sociology*, 4, 171–7

Tufts, J. H. 1896. Recent sociological tendencies in France. In *American Journal of Sociology*, 1, 446–56

Turner, S. 1983–4. Durkheim as a methodologist. In *Philosophy of the Social Sciences*, 13, 425–50; 14, 51–71

Wallwork, E. 1972. *Durkheim, Morality and Milieu*, Cambridge, Mass., Harvard University Press

Wood, M. 1978. Marcel Mauss. In *New Society*, 43 (19 Jan.) 124–6

Name Index

Aimard, G., 90–1
Alexander, J., 67, 100–1
Althusser, L., 157
Alpert, H., 68, 96–7, 99
Aristotle, 26, 29, 59, 82, 124
Ashworth, C., 71

Bachelard, G., 71, 182
Bacon, F., 134, 135, 142, 147
Baldwin, J., 95
Balibar, E., 157
Bayet, A., 97
Benton, T., 70, 173
Bataille, G., 89
Bergson, H., 76, 95
Besnard, P., 75, 108, 115, 157
Bougle, C., 4, 41, 75
Bourdieu, P., 183
Bryant, C., 73, 169

Canguilhem, G., 182
Caillois, R., 89
Catlin, G., 12, 95
Clarke, T. N., 75, 76, 80
Comte, A., 14, 17, 18, 26, 34, 37, 38,
   41, 46, 59, 60, 61, 82, 88, 90, 91,
   102, 122
Condorcet, Marquis de, 26, 41, 124
Cooley, C., 95, 97

Dandeker, C., 71
Davis, K., 99
Davy, G., 107
Descartes, R., 22, 28, 38, 100, 134,
   135, 156, 181
Deploige, S., 81–3, 173

Diderot, D., 124

Engels, F., 61
Erasmus, 52
Espinas, A., 27, 82

Fauconnet, P., 30, 35–8, 59, 127
Fechner, G.-T., 146
Fenton, S., 2, 123
Filloux, J.-C., 91, 157
Fletcher, R., 69
Fouillee, A., 84–5, 94
Foucault, G., 182
Fourier, C., 38

Gane, M., 59, 60, 111, 159, 176
Gehlke, G., 94–5
Giddens, A., 2, 5, 50, 67, 68, 69, 71,
   100
Giddings, F., 37, 95
Gisbert, P., 99–100
Goffman, E., 4
Gramsci, A., 176
Gurvitch, G., 90, 157

Halbwachs, M., 41, 53
Hegel, G. W. F., 90
Hertz, R., 59
Hirst, P., 71–2, 157, 169, 170, 173
Hobbes T., 18
Hubert, H., 41, 59, 179

Ihering, R. von, 27
Izoulet, J., 75

James, W., 95
Janet, P., 32

Name Index

Johnson, T., 71
Jones, R. A., 2

Kant, I., 40, 91, 104
Keat, R., 73–4
Kolakowski, L., 73

LaCapra, D., 100
Lacroix, B., 67, 91–2, 157, 158, 172, 178
Lang, A., 94
Lee, D., 69
Letourneau, C., 27, 41, 183
Lukes, S., 2, 7, 12, 21, 56, 57, 61, 62, 67, 74, 76, 78, 100, 123, 153, 155, 165–7, 170, 171, 178

Maire, G., 7
Marshall, G., 99, 173, 182
Marx, K., 1, 28, 60, 61, 86, 90, 181
Mauss, M., 4, 30, 35–7, 41, 59, 90, 108, 127, 137, 163, 164, 176, 178, 179
Merleau-Ponty, M., xv, 183
Merton, R. K., 99
Mill, J. S., 18, 37, 164
Montaigne, M. E. de, 52
Montesquieu, C.-L. de Secdondat, 26, 27, 29, 41, 59

Needham, R., 175
Newby, H., 69
Nisbet, R. A., 3, 12, 68, 99, 100

Parsons, T., 67, 68, 96–9
Pascal, B., 26, 227, 259
Passeron, J.-C., 183
Peyre, H., 5
Pickering, W. S. F., 2, 107
Pope, W., 99, 109

Post, A., 27

Rabelais, F., 52
Renouvier, C., 83
Rex, J., 70
Ricoeur, P., 160
Roche, M., 8–11

Sahlins, M., 68, 170
Saint Simon, C. H. de, 30, 38, 41, 60, 61, 62, 113, 122
Schaeffle, A., 22, 27
Schmidt, J., 183
Schmaus, W., 4, 101–2, 165
Schmoller, G., 27
Seignobos, C., 83–4
Shils, E., 99
Simiand, F., 41
Simmel, G., 33, 37, 91
Smart, B., 73
Smith, W. Robertson, 82
Sorel, G., 75, 85, 86, 95
Spencer, H., 14, 17, 18, 27, 37, 59, 82, 88

Tarde, G., 27, 28, 67, 76–81, 88, 90, 91, 94, 95, 120, 160, 182
Tarde, G. de, 80
Tosti, G., 93
Tufts, J. H., 93
Turner, S., 101

Urry, J., 73–4

Wagner, A., 27
Wallwork, E., 5, 6, 43, 100, 123
Warner, W. L., 99
Weber, M., 91, 96, 100
Wood, M., 4

Subject Index

abnormal, *see* normal
absolutism, 47
accumulation, strategic/historical, 39, 175, 180–1
anarchism, 6, 19, 20, 61, 94, 121
analysis, by analogy, 177; functional, 60, 95, 99, 101, 163–4; genetic/generic, 163, 179; structural, 37, 133, 164, 177
Annee Sociologique, 1, 20, 30, 41, 67, 83, 111, 130
anomie, 45, 53, 108
authoritarianism, 9, 11

bourgeoisie, 6

Cartesianism, 22, 156
categories, 40, 55, 121
cause and effect, 39, 60, 163; gap between 165; mechanical cause, 44, 48
classification, 17, 24, 26, 29, 35, 42, 50, 58, 121, 145, 163, 174
collective representations, 32, 40, 55, 100, 123, 160
communism, 6, 19, 119
comparative series and induction, 36, 37, 44, 49, 54, 56
complexity, idea of in Durkheim, 4, 26, 29, 37, 41, 60, 85, 91, 103–4, 108, 182; causal complexity, 163; discipline as complex, 121; complex effects, 51; complex rationalism, 38; social complexity, 122, 175; strategic complexity, 6, 115

conditions necessary for the emergence of sociology, 28, 41, 182
controversial, the, 125; removal of, 174
contradiction, 116; and dialectic, 121
conscience collective, 62, 87, 89, 113, 153, 157
corporations, 61
crime and punishment, 16, 43–9, 128–9
cult, 56–7; state and, 122
currents, social, 14, 25, 139, 144

definitions, 35, 36, 44, 50, 70, 88, 96, 115, 131, 143, 147, 155
density, dynamic, 18, 24, 92, 101, 112–3
dialectic, 5, 6, 40, 121, 125; and definitions, 147; suppression of, 177
dialogue on the Rules (Roche), 8–11
divisions of sociology, 23, 30, 37, 39, 41, 108
discipline, 35, 119, 121
domain of sociology, 137–41
Durkheim, E., sociology: as ambiguous, 74, 104; not ambiguous, 35; apriorist, 88, 90; conservative, 5, 118, 119; as contradictory, 3, 68–70, 165, 170; not contradictory, 116–7; not eclectic, 114; empiricist, 69–70, 90, 143, 168f; not empiricist, 40, 168–70; essentialist, 74, 86; idealist, not idealist; 168; not introspectionist, 30, 134, 169; moralist, 82, 88; not

Durkheim, E., sociology—*cont.*
materialist, 168; mystic, 24, 78–80, 90; positivist, 24, 72, 98, 168; rationalist, 71; realist, 71, 97, 98, 102; not realist, 114, 168; subjectivist, 90, 101; substantialist, 156, not substantialist; scientistic, 69

major works: *Division*, 23, 43–4, 76, 98, 100, 107, 110, 112, 126–8, 146, 158, 161, 164, 165, 169, 177; *Rules*, ix, xi, 2, 7, 8, 12–20, 21, 25, 33, 98, 99, 101, 108, 111, 113, 118, 122, 137f, 152f; *Suicide*, 49–51, 79, 88, 107, 110, 146, 157, 168, 178; *Educational Thought*, 51–3, 123f, 162, 178; Forms, 53–8, 108, 110, 112, 162, 165, 177, 180

minor works: 'Review of Schaeffle', (1885), 22; 'Introduction to the sociology of the family', (1888), 22–4; 'Suicide and birth rates', (1888), 24–5; 'Opening lecture', 25, 130; 'Lectures on socialism', (1895–6), 27; 'Sociology in France', (in Italian, 1895), 27; 'Montesquieu', (in Latin, 1892), 29; 'Moral education', (1898), 120; 'Individual and collective representations', (1898), 30, 31; 'Sociology in France', (1900), 30, 38; 'Sociology and its scientific domain', (1900), 30, 33, 130; 'On the objective method in sociology', (1901), 30, 130; 'Sociology and social sciences' (with Fauconnet, 1903); 'Moral facts', (1906), 112, 130, 167; 'Sociology and social sciences', (1909), 39; 'Sociology of religion and sociology of knowledge', (1909), 40; 'Sociology', 41; 'Ethics', (1917), 41, 85; 'Germany Above All', (1915), 41

efficient cause, 17, 44, 60, 91, 147, 164
energy, social and causation, 156, 159

evolution, social, 26–7, 29, 51, 54, 179
experiment, 24, 29, 44, 53–4, 149, 174, 179, 180

family, analysis of, 23, 24, 39, 46, 127, 159
fascism, 95, 176
focus, of research, 131, 135–6
form and content, 33–4, 54
function, 23, 45
France, 5, 172–4; education in, 51, 120, 180; sociology in, 28, 38, 41

general sociology, 37, 39
God, 56, 88

history and evolution, 39, 53, 83, 175, 179
holism, 3, 20, 45, 72, 108, 154
humanism, 19, 62

imitation, 28, 76–77
individual, 14, 40, 48, 62, 77–81, 83, 85, 95, 97, 140, 152, 155, 158; in science, 122; individual form, 51; type, 141, 146
institutional socialism, 61
interference, between theses in *Rules*, 143, 153
inventories, 127, 131, 138, 148, 172

Jesuits, 123–4

materialisation, 113
materialism, 29, 32, 35, 86, 157, 116
material causation, 130
Marxism, 28, 60, 75, 85–6, 91
monism, 117
morality, 5, 41, 43, 85, 88, 132, 134
morphology and physiology, 17, 18, 34–5, 57, 111, 112, 117, 148

normal and pathological, 15, 24, 29, 45, 88, 132, 145f

observation, 70, 124, 134, 141, 145

objectivity, 28–9
order of study, 48, 50, 116
order of explanation, 148
positivism, 24, 27, 168
power, 158–60
prenotion, 134–5, 143–4, 168, 177
proofs, 18, 25, 46, 149
project, Durkheim's 7, 20, 40, 55, 62, 109, 113, 115, 122, 127, 129, 173, 179

rationalism, 19, 22, 28, 38, 41, 181
reading, Durkheim on, 3–11
reductionism, 28, 32, 115
religion, 53–4, 86, 109, 111, 122, 159, 162, 165
rhetoric, 123
Renaissance, 52–3, 61, 123, 180
revolutionary, Durkheim as, 5, 19, 63, 118, 177

sanction and norm, 25, 128, 129, 131
sensation, 48, 55, 142–4, 167, 169
science, 8, 32, 38, 42; authority of, 120; categories, 121; causality, 25, 44, 115–6; discipline, 119, 121; and ideal, 121; and morality, 58; as unique object, 137; tolerance, 122; and social categories, 58
social environment (milieu), 18, 34, 86, 92, 140, 148, 162
social fact, external sign of, 25, 29, 33, 42, 55, 112; external to individuals, 13; generality of, 14, 16, 139; as ideal, 130–3;

independent of individual forms, 14, 88; interiority, 33, 55, 58, 112; no absolute definition of, 131, 154; and moral facts, 127–8; primary and derived, 33, 57
socialism, 6, 61
sociology, as French discipline, 38; lineage of, 23, 26, 38, 41, 59, 82
sociology, and philosophy, 40, 88; and psychology, 31–2, 40, 117, 160–1, 160–3
sociology of knowledge, 53, 57, 175
solidarity, 23, 108
spirituality, principle of, 4, 29, 91, 114, 116, 117
statics and dynamics, 49, 162, 179–80
strategy, Durkheim's intellectual, 6–7, 40, 42, 55, 107, 113f, 115, 120f, 149–50, 171; criticisms of, 177–81; and politics, 173–4
suicide, 24, 129, 164, 174, 178

theory, 46, 70
thing, treat social fact as, 14, 15, 31, 133–4
transition, simple and complex, 118–125, 133
truth, 20, 121, 124–5

unconscious, the, 32
utilitarianism, 98, 104

verstehen, 110, 166
violence, 52